PASTORAL RESPONSES TO OLDER ADULTS AND THEIR FAMILIES

PASTORAL RESPONSES TO OLDER ADULTS AND THEIR FAMILIES

An Annotated Bibliography

Compiled by
Henry C. Simmons
and
Vivienne S. Pierce

BV
4580
.S56x
1992
WEST

Bibliographies and Indexes in Gerontology, Number 15
Erdman B. Palmore, Series Adviser

GREENWOOD PRESS
New York • Westport, Connecticut • London

Library of Congress Cataloging-in-Publication Data

Simmons, Henry C.
　Pastoral responses to older adults and their families : an
annotated bibliography / compiled by Henry C. Simmons and Vivienne
S. Pierce.
　　p.　cm.—(Bibliographies and indexes in gerontology, ISSN
0743-7560 ; no. 15)
　Includes indexes.
　ISBN 0-313-28039-8 (alk. paper)
　1. Aged—Religious life—Bibliography.　2. Aged—Pastoral
counseling of—Bibliography.　3. Aged—Bibliography.　I. Pierce,
Vivienne S.　II. Title.　III. Series.
Z7761.S55　1992
[BV4580]
016.259'3—dc20　　　91-43560

British Library Cataloguing in Publication Data is available.

Library of Congress Catalog Card Number: 91-43560
ISBN: 0-313-28039-8
ISSN: 0743-7560

First published in 1992

Greenwood Press, 88 Post Road West, Westport, CT 06881
An imprint of Greenwood Publishing Group, Inc.

Printed in the United States of America

The paper used in this book complies with the
Permanent Paper Standard issued by the National
Information Standards Organization (Z39.48-1984).

10 9 8 7 6 5 4 3 2 1

For Harold J. and Miriam J. Pierce, and Adrienne J. Fleming

and

Helen C. McDonald

Contents

Series Foreword

The annotated bibliographies in this series provide answers to the fundamental question, "What is known?" Their purpose is simple, yet profound: to provide comprehensive reviews and references for the work done in various fields of gerontology. They are based on the fact that it is no longer possible for anyone to comprehend the vast body of research and writing in even one sub-specialty without years of work.

This fact has become true only in recent years. When I was an undergraduate (Class of '52) I think no one at Duke had even heard of gerontology. Almost no one in the world was identified as a gerontologist. Now there are over 6,000 professional members of the Gerontological Society of America. When I was an undergraduate there were no courses in gerontology. Now there are thousands of courses offered by most major (and many minor) colleges and universities. When I was an undergraduate there was only one gerontological journal (Journal of Gerontology, begun in 1945). Now there are over 40 professional journals and several dozen books in gerontology published each year.

The reasons for this dramatic growth are well known: the increase in numbers of aged, the shift from family to public responsibility for the security and care of the elderly, the recognition of aging as a "social problem," and the growth of science in general. It is less well known that this explosive growth in knowledge has developed the need for new solutions to the old problem of comprehending and "keeping up" with a field of knowledge. The old indexes and library card catalogs have become increasingly inadequate for the job. On-line computer indexes and abstracts are one solution but they make no evaluative selections nor do they organize sources logically as is done in this bibliography. Annotated bibliographies are also more widely available than online computer indexes.

These bibliographies will obviously be useful for researchers who need to know what research has (or has not) been done in their field. The annotations contain enough information so that the researcher usually does not have to search out the original articles. In the past, the "review of literature" has often been haphazard and was rarely comprehensive, because of the large investment of time (and money) that would be required by a truly comprehensive review. Now, using these bibliographies, researchers can be confident that they are not missing important previous research; they can be confident that they are not duplicating past efforts and "reinventing the wheel." It may well become standard and expected practice for researchers to consult such bibliographies, before they start their research.

Religion is one of the most important areas within gerontology for several reasons: most elders belong to a church or synagogue; elders make up the largest age group in many congregations; the proportion of elders in most congregations will probably increase in the next few years; churches and synagogues are becoming more aware of the special needs and resources of their elder members; and religion is more important to elders than it is to younger generations. Thus, a comprehensive bibliography in this area is one of the most important in gerontology.

This book is needed not only by academics, students, and researchers, but also by pastoral professionals and lay-persons who work with elders, by elders themselves, and by anyone who wants to better understand elders. Indeed, the items included were selected and annotated with non-academics in mind.

The authors have done an outstanding job of covering all the relevant literature and organizing it into an easily accessible form. Not only are there 736 annotated references organized into 10 chapters and 21 sub-sections, but there are also a preface, an introductory chapter, an author index, and a subject index with many cross-references to the items in the bibliography.

One can look for relevant material in this volume in several ways: (1) look up a given subject in the subject index; (2) look up a given author in the author index; (3) turn to the section that covers the topic; or (4) look over the introduction for a basic orientation to the topic.

Dr. Simmons is unusually qualified to author this bibliography because of his years of experience as teacher and writer in the area of gerontology (the bibliography annotates 17 of his publications). He has been ably assisted by his coauthor Vivienne S. Pierce. Also, they (together with Barbara Payne) are the authors of a previous brief bibliography on "Theology and Aging" (1988). Their entries are concise and clear so that one can easily understand the main contents of the reference and decide whether the original is worth pursuing.

So it is with great pleasure that we add this bibliography to our series. We believe you will find this volume to be the most useful, comprehensive, and easily accessible reference work in its field.   I will appreciate any comments you care to send me.

Erdman B. Palmore
Center for the Study of Aging and Human Development
Box 3003, Duke University Medical Center
Durham, NC 27710

Preface

This comprehensive bibliography of 736 items is intended, in the first place, for practicing clergy, educators, lay professionals, and laity. It will also be of use in the selection of texts and preparation of courses in seminaries. For professional gerontologists interested in relgion and aging, it will help identify areas of concern in communities of faith.

Clergy, educators, lay professionals, and laity form an audience distinct from other audiences addressed by gerontological bibliographies. There are, of course, areas of overlap. For example, a bibliography on death and dying would list many items of interest within communities of faith. Nevertheless, the interest of the local congregation, its leaders and adherents, is specified by its own needs and goals, by its way of functioning, and by its general lack of sophistication in social science literature. A unique contribution of the bibliography is its organization of the field of religion and aging from a pastoral perspective.

Studies of aging may be approached both from humanities perspectives and from social science perspectives. This bibliography is located within the humanities. Without exception, its entries can be read without a technical background in the social sciences.

This bibliography will also be of use in the selection of texts and preparation of courses in seminaries. Relatively few such courses are presently taught and few seminary professors have a background in gerontology. This bibliography, organized in a fashion that will be perceived as "user friendly" by teachers in seminaries, fills a specific need. It allows these teachers to read wisely in a variety of areas and to integrate gerontological material into their courses and curricula.

For professional gerontologists interested in religion and aging, this bibliography helps identify areas of concern in communities of faith. It also helps them to organize their own knowledge and skills in appropriate ways in their presentations to religious professionals and church/synagogue congregations. The areas covered by this bibliography include Church and Synagogue; Empowerment; Ethics; Personal Spiritual Life; Life Review and Written Reminiscences; Death and Dying; Theology, Bible, and other Religions; Religious Professionals; Special Populations; and Health and Religion.

Note in the text that the Journal of Religion and Aging and Journal of Religious Gerontology are the same. The journal name was changed to the latter beginning with volume 7.

Acknowledgments

We are grateful to several people whose efforts made this bibliography possible. The staff of the Union Theological Seminary Library was most helpful. In particular, Patsy Verreault, Reference Librarian, performed the data base searches from which the bibliography was, in part, compiled. She also worked especially hard to fill an unusually large volume of interlibrary loan requests. Melanie Towb, a graduate student assistant at the Center on Aging, joined in our project with great enthusiasm. She did library research, looked up and photocopied articles, tracked down books, filled in interlibrary loan request slips, picked up materials from the library--in short, did all sorts of jobs that are both indispensable and too easily forgotten. We appreciate her generous contribution. Harlan ("Mac") McMurray, who seems to be on better terms with computers than most, helped with technical short-cuts. Dr. Erdman B. Palmore, Series Advisor for Greenwood Press's Bibliographies and Indexes in Gerontology Series, asked us to undertake this project. We appreciate his invitation. Finally, we are grateful for the support of our academic institution, the Presbyterian School of Christian Education. From 1978 to 1979, Dr. Albert E. Dimmock and Ms. Louise McComb began the collection and organization of resources in ministry with older adults. Since then the Center on Aging of this school has been responsible for teaching, researching, and resourcing in the area of religion and aging. The present work stands within a long history of institutional commitment to older adults.

Abbreviations

AARP	American Association of Retired Persons
AGHE	Association of Gerontology in Higher Education
DAI	Dissertation Abstracts International
Ed. and Eds.	Editor/Editors
ERIC	Educational Resources Information Center
n.d.	No date
NTIS	National Technical Information Service
PCUS	Presbyterian Church, U.S.
SWB	Spiritual Well-Being
WHCoA	White House Conference on Aging

Introduction

Nowhere is the graying of America more evident than in churches and synagogues. The proportion of older adults among their congregants far exceeds national norms. Nowhere is the responsiveness of America to its older adults more a possibility than in churches and synagogues. Churches and synagogues are the places where older adults, younger adults, families, and children most frequently and intimately come face to face. Churches and synagogues have places, even perhaps officially recognized places and functions, for elders. Churches and synagogues are places where people have traditionally looked to make friends, to help out, to be together for the most important moments of life. Churches and synagogues are places of responsiveness to older adults and their families.

This annotated bibliography has several principal purposes. First, it signals that pastoral responsiveness to elders and their families has been and is a notable dimension of the life of religious groups. In many ways this bibliography is a record of the richness and inventiveness of the interaction between younger and older in communities of faith. Second, this bibliography signals the need to be more inventive, more responsive, more comprehensive in our responses to elders and their families. In many ways it is a challenge to expand and enrich--to add service to words of care, to add strategies of empowerment to care for the frail, to add ethical inquiry to personal devotion, to add liturgical expression to religious education, to add advocacy to hospice and adult day-care. Third, this bibliography signals the need for research--theoretical, programmatic, applied. In many ways it has become evident that work in this area is spotty and that there have been far too many "reinventions of the wheel."

While this bibliography is the most comprehensive and up-to-date of its kind, it is not the first bibliography in the area of religion and aging. Other bibliographies, in chronological order, include: "Bibliography: Spiritual Well-being" [not annotated], David O. Moberg, 1971; "Summaries of Books relevant to the Topic of Spirituality and Aging," Carolyn Gratton, 1980; Religion and the Aging: A Bibliography [not annotated], North Texas State University, 1981; Religion and Aging: An Annotated Bibliography, Vincent John Fecher, 1982. Fecher's bibliography was, until the present work, the only book-length annotated bibliography in religion and aging. It is still an important work, worthy of consultation. "Bibliography: Religion and Aging," Thomas C. Cook, Jr., 1983; "Bibliography on Aging for Pastors and Other Church Leaders," David O. Moberg, 1987; Theology and Aging, AGHE Brief Bibliography, Henry C. Simmons, Vivienne Walaskay, Barbara Payne, 1988; "Gerontology and Religion: An Annotated Bibliography," Barbara Payne, 1989; and "Sources and Resources," Henry C. Simmons, 1990.

Other more general bibliographies have included sections on religion, ethics, church programs and services. Again in chronological order, these bibliographies include: Aging in the Modern World, Office of Aging, H.E.W , 1963; Words on aging: A Bibliography, Office of Human Development, AoA, 1970; Where Do We Come From? What Are We? Where Are We Going?, Donna Polisar et al., Gerontological Society of America, 1988.

Within the limited scope of this bibliography, we have tried to be as comprehensive as possible. In addition to consulting the above-mentioned bibliographies, we searched Religious Books, 1876-1982, Religious & Inspirational Books & Serials in Print (1978-1979, 1985) and Books in Print. An extensive computer search was undertaken in March of 1991. The following computerized data bases were searched: ERIC, Dissertation Abstracts International Online, Social Science Index, and NTIS. Much recent material on religion and aging was found in two journals: Journal of Religion and Aging (now Journal of Religious Gerontology) and Journal of Judaism and Aging. Each issue of each journal was examined, from its beginning (Fall, 1984 and Fall/Winter, 1986 respectively) to May of 1991. Finally, the resource collection of the Center on Aging of the Presbyterian School of Christian Education of Richmond, Virginia, was a valuable asset in the identification of important materials.

ORGANIZATION OF THE TEXT

We began this annotated bibliography with a fairly detailed outline which, in part, guided our search for materials. The outline was logical, following a schematization which seemed clear and consistent. The outline served its purposes in our identification of materials. But it has not proved particularly useful in putting in order the materials actually collected. There were materials in areas where we had anticipated none; more often there were too few materials to form a chapter in areas where logic dictated that there be a well-developed corpus. Further, as we sorted material we realized that a logic of use had its own importance. We need to keep in mind the reader who wants to find what has been written on a particular topic without knowing in advance the key words which have been used for organization.

Thus, the logic of division of material in this annotated bibliography is twofold: materials available and presumed use. By "materials available" we mean that we took all the references we thought useful to include and tried to see patterns within that vast array. By "presumed use" we mean that we have tried to envision how the reader might choose to look for materials in this bibliography. For example, we have a separate chapter called "Death and Dying" not because this is a logically coherent collection of writings (indeed the approaches and disciplines of this area are quite disparate) but because we thought that death and dying was a point of reference a reader might well presume.

We trust that our division of the materials will prove helpful to the user. We also hope that persons who choose to write in the general area covered by this bibliography will have a keen eye for areas which need development or connections which need to be forged.

The text is organized into ten chapters, very uneven in length: Church and Synagogue; Empowerment; Ethics; Personal Spiritual Life; Life Review and Written Reminiscences; Death and Dying; Theology, Bible, and Other Religions; Religious Professionals; Special Populations; and Health and Religion.

1. Church and Synagogue

In this chapter are gathered materials related to the pastoral response of local churches and synagogues (and in some cases slightly larger denominational bodies) to elders in their midst or in their care. The first section presents comprehensive guides to ministry with the aging, the second and third offer specific programs and models or approaches to ministry from particular perspectives (sociology, pastoral care, etc.) The fourth section addresses the response of the local church and synagogue to elders in its midst in worship and ritual. Section five looks to educational programs for awareness and enrichment (in distinction to programs for a specific issue or task). Section six inquires about the place of the church or synagogue in the community service system and in the personal networks of elders. Finally, section seven looks to the institutional care of the aged as a response of church or synagogue and the care of those who are institutionalized.

All these sections are characterized by a sense of immediacy of presence of elders to others in the church or synagogue and by a sense of communality in approach and relationship. Sometimes the elder is seen as one to be cared for; less often the elder is seen as agent. In part this is because of the arrangement of this bibliography, which separates "Empowerment" from "Church and Synagogue."

Comprehensive Guides to Ministry

The principal characteristic of the items in this section is their comprehensiveness. They tend (and intend) to be complete manuals for use in congregations as these congregations plan for and engage in ministry to, with, and for older adults. These are practical manuals--what you need to know to plan older adult ministry and actually do that ministry. Typically, these books present a menu to select from, rather than advocating one particular approach. Articles in this section are of course less comprehensive, but they too are practical guides to older adult ministry.

Some of the issues that these materials might typically include are: demographics, characteristics of the elderly, religious needs and strengths, participation and barriers to participation, categories or types of older adults (well, less active, homebound, institutionalized), objectives of older adult ministries, types of ministry (worship, education, service and volunteering, social, advocacy, personal development, cooperation with social services, religious programming, pastoral care, social service).

Specific Programs and Models

In this section are included programs built around specific issues and model programs. In the first category are a wide variety of lay training programs for specific ministries, a number of programs for adults with aging parents, and other items as specific as counseling older adults considering remarriage. In the category of model programs are a variety of programs actually run successfully, presented with great specificity (e.g. Senior Tuesdays, The Jolly Sixties, The Retired Club).

Programs from Particular Perspectives

In this section are gathered materials which look at church programming from one or another perspective: e.g., sociology, church growth, pastoral psychology, mental health, adult development, Scripture, cultural and social inquiry. In most cases, what distinguishes these programs and gives them their specificity is the profession of the author: the sociologist takes a different slant from the pastoral psychologist, etc.

Worship, Ritual, Preaching, and Hymns

The material in this section encompasses worship and prayer-in-common. In most items it is presumed that people are gathered together to worship God. The settings vary from convalescent home, to home, to church or synagogue. Worship is usually understood to affect not only one's relationship with God but also with the community of worship. Hence worship which is sensitively inclusive can build or rebuild bonds between the generations and among elders.

Several items in this section are related specifically to the study of ritual. These are included to suggest ways in which persons planning worship might more sensitively create appropriate ways of doing what ritual accomplishes at its best--living forward into the hoped-for order.

Educational Programs for Awareness and Enrichment

In this section are educational programs whose purpose is to enrich the lives of participants. "Enrichment" distinguishes these programs from programs which are more oriented to issue or task (lay ministry training, for example). Some of these programs are comprehensive (for example, Affirmative Aging) while others are specific. There is a variety of educational materials gathered in this section: elementary and secondary school education on aging, films and videos on Judaism and aging, Bible education with older adults.

Social Services

Items found in this section relate to the place of the church or synagogue in the community service system and in the personal networks of elders. Many of these books and articles assume that the role of the religious institution is to connect with and support community service systems; others inquire about specific social service programs which can be initiated in and by a church or synagogue (adult day care or respite care, for example).

Institutional Care of the Aged

This section contains books and articles which assume that the older adult is in an institutional setting: nursing home, hospital, long-term care facility, church- or synagogue-related homes. With this as the common factor, the subject is approached from a variety of perspectives: organizational behavior, pastoral care, friendly visiting, Bible study, ethics, recreation and creative activities, education, and so on.

2. Empowerment

Writings in this chapter focus on the empowerment of older adults. Empowerment may be understood as something which happens within groups of individuals; one cannot empower another, although one may facilitate the process. At the same time, most of these writings have a collective sense: they assume that although an individual might empower himself or herself, it is more likely that this will happen with the support and facilitation of a group. Issues of empowerment may deal with organizing for legislative activity, retirement home organization, personal and collective freedom, economics, ministries, facing death and life, and so on.

A single item in this chapter, namely an issue of Generations, "Low Technology for Maximizing Independence," addresses issues of independence through appropriate technology.

3. Ethics

In general, ethics is concerned with what is good and right. A specific ethical question is one which asks what it is good and right to do in a particular case. The answer to a specific ethical question informs the questioner, on the basis of a practical, intellectual decision, what is to be done in the here and now. Ethics, understood in this sense, is first order discourse which provides practical guidelines. In the present bibliography, ethics includes writings that provide practical guidelines in regard to older adults.

Popular writing on ethics and aging may lead to a focus on dramatic issues in biomedical ethics, an enormously complex field of inquiry which has developed its own extensive literature. (See Bibliography of Bioethics, Washington, DC: Kennedy Institute of Ethics, Georgetown University. Volume 16 is edited by LeRoy Walters and Tamar Joy Kahn.) Some of the materials which we have collected in this chapter discuss Jewish or Christian positions regarding the donation of organs, autopsy, treatment decisions for the elderly, and so on. But the scope of ethical inquiry turns out to be much broader than bioethics. Our materials have been divided into five groups.

General and Specific Ethical Questions

"General and specific ethical questions" is, as noted, perhaps the least tidy of the sections on ethics. Some of the articles deal with general ethical norms (what might be termed principles of ethics); others ask specific ethical questions (where principles are applied to practice), which are placed here because they do not fall into any of the categories which follow. The reader will note that many of them address questions of medical ethics. Two collections are placed in this section because some of the essays are in the area of philosophy and ethics. Others of the essays implicitly address questions of the right and good, although it would probably be clearer to group these essays under the large rubric of interdisciplinary humanities.

Ethics in the Public Domain

"Ethics in the public domain" groups materials on questions of public policy, the distribution of resources, Medicare and, more broadly, public images of elders and the public consequence of these images. Part of the focus of this section is on ethical issues in public policy for older adults and their families: issues like income support programs, Medicare, long-term care, elder housing, the use of high-technology anti-aging techniques. The second part of this section focuses on the perception of elders in society and the way in which public negative perceptions qualify them for diminished access to the resources of society.

Filial Responsibility

"Filial responsibility" inquires about the responsibility of adult children for their aging parents in the light of a variety of factors: the obligation of the individual to make some preparation for retirement and old age, the legal obligations of the family towards elderly parents, the diversity of actors and roles, family decision-making, the political sphere in which these questions are decided. Other materials approach the question less from the orientation of who has the responsibility for providing care than from a growth perspective: what adult children should do to understand, care for, and cope with aging parents.

Termination of Life

"Termination of life" deals with questions of suicide, euthanasia, and the prolongation of life. Some items take a historical approach to these ethical issues; others begin from specific Jewish or Christian perspectives. Materials were chosen for this section because they appeared in religious journals, were denominationally specific, and/or appeared under religion and aging in computer searches. What is here is a mere trace of the literature written on these subjects.

Right Ways to Be an Older Adult

"Right ways to be an older adult" is comprised of books, pamphlets, and articles which have to do with a variety of realities: retirement, marriage, grandparenting, health-care and nutrition, finances, volunteering. These writings are distinguised from their secular counterparts because of an explicit appeal to religious values, they have appeared in religious or denominational publications, or they were produced by a religious or denominational press. We have placed these publications under ethics because in each case something prescriptive is is being proposed: one should approach this or that particular reality in this or that way. In our understanding, these are ethical responses to a variety of life situations: they have to do with practical guidelines about what it is good and right to do in a specific aspect of life.

This section is divided into two parts, depending on the age of the writers. Where authors have identified themselves as seniors, we have placed their writings in the section Right Ways to Be an Older Adult: Author Identified as a Senior. Where authors have not identified themselves as seniors or their age is not known, we have placed their writings in the section Right Ways to Be an Older Adult: Authors Not Identified as a Senior.   Many of these writings could also be classed as devotional. We have been attentive in assessing devotional books to ask the question whether the primary emphasis is on one's relationship to God (in which case we list the book under "Personal Religious Life") or on one's response to God's will (in which case the book is placed in this section). Some books fall without question into this category-- religion seems only to be a veneer; prescriptions for how to live are drawn from other, secular sources, although there is usually some appeal to religious realities.

4. Personal Spiritual Life

This chapter includes books of meditations, books and articles on the devout life, materials on spiritual development and growth, and materials on spiritual well-being. Books and articles on the devout life are further divided into those in which the author is identified as a senior and those in which this is not the case. This chapter does not include church and synagogue programs for development of the spiritual life or worship and liturgy. Virtually all of the devotional material of this chapter is tied to a specific religion and denomination. The material on spiritual well-being tends to be broader and the section on spiritual development and growth contains material from a variety of perspectives.

Meditations

The more than forty books in this section indicate that this type of literature plays a significant part in the personal spiritual life of many Christians. Typically, these books stress a positive view of life, encourage service of God and humanity, and include "consolation" as one of their purposes. The titles of these books taken together give a fairly accurate picture of their thrust and orientation. About one in five of these books is a translation. On the whole--although there are clear exceptions--translated books tend to have a more substantial feel; this probably reflects their selection as worthy of translation.

All the literature in this section is Christian. Although there is Jewish representation in virtually every other category, none of the books of meditations is by a Jew. Jews are, however, disproportionately represented in some sections of ethics. Perhaps these differences offer insight into the function of the personal devotional life of some Christians.

The Devout Life

The materials in this section range from the commonsensical and inspirational to the literary and philosophical. Much of the material seems, with the perspective of time, to have little lasting value; yet some of the material is of such depth and clarity that it has enduring urgency. The more light weight material is kept for its importance to the student of the subject, and some pieces are saved, frankly, as horrible examples. All the materials presented are explicitly Christian and use some particular language of Christian faith to help the reader reflect on, make sense of, wonder about, and live life. Literary forms include sermons, devotional texts, pamphlets, conferences, and lectures.

We had some hesitation about dividing this block of literature on the basis of age. In the end we decided to go ahead with the decision in order to respect the self-identification of the author as being a certain age as well as to alert other researchers to inquire what specific differences, if any, age makes to content or style. We do not claim that an author is not a senior but simply that the author is not identified as a senior.

Spiritual Development and Growth

What holds this section together is a concern for the increase or flowering of the human spirit at a time of life when loss is probable. We also note, although this was not a principle of selection, that most items use some metaphor which could be interpreted as spatial or visual: movement or growth, development or journey, maturity or depth. Despite communalities, this is not a particularly tidy section, partly because of the variety of disciplines involved: developmental psychology, humanistic psychology, psychoanalysis, literary analysis, theology, mysticism, philosophy, art. It is also untidy because some items have found their way here simply because this was where they seemed least out of place.

Spiritual Well-Being

The term "spiritual well-being" was used in the 1971 White House Conference on Aging, and taken up by the National Interfaith Coalition on Aging with the following definition: "the affirmation of life in a relationship with God, self, community and environment that nurtures and celebrates wholeness" (James A. Thorson and Thomas C. Cook, Eds., Spiritual Well-Being of the Elderly, Springfield, IL: Charles C. Thomas, 1980, p. xiii). In this section are gathered materials which use this term explicitly. Some of the material relates directly to the history of the term over the past decades, some of the material uses this term as a research construct or for the construction of a scale of measurement.

5. Life Review and Written Reminiscences

Included in this part of the bibliography are materials on life-review-- materials which help people find patterns in and make sense of memories and written reminiscences, including journals, autobiographies, and biographies.

Life Review

This section gathers materials which in some manner or other focus on finding patterns in and making sense of memories. Memories are key to all these writings, with memory understood in a dynamic way as open to reinterpretation and reintegration into the persons's present. A variety of approaches emerge: story-telling, journal writing, logotherapy, structured life-review processes, self-narratives. This section of literature is notable for its richness and its consistency.

Written Reminiscences

This section includes journals, autobiographies, and biographies. The journals and autobiographies are of interest not only for the insights one may gain into another's life but also as models for other people to follow in writing about their own lives. Thus, they may have an educational dimension.

6. Death and Dying

The logic of gathering the following references into one section is found in the topic rather than in the approach. While each item addresses death or dying, the disciplines represented include theology, sociology, poetry, philosophy, biography, literature, and devotional literature.

The inclusion of death and dying in this bibliography is problematic: death can happen in any decade of human life. Yet, in our culture death is more likely to happen in old age than at any other time of life. The more people die in old age the more likely the culture will associate advanced age with death. Thus we decided to include a very modest amount of literature on death and dying. What is found here should be considered at best a small sample of a very broad literature.

7. Theology, Bible, Other Religions

In this section we gather materials from two disciplines, each of which has its own scholarly methods of research and inquiry: theology and the Bible. The third item, other religions, includes materials from sources other than Judaism and Christianity.

Theology

The distinguishing characteristic of the materials in this section is that they use a specifically theological methodology (indeed, most, although not all of the authors would identify themselves as professional theologians). Some of the items are systematic attempts to create a "theology of aging," while others address specific subjects (e.g. theodicy, spirituality, meaning, Rabbinic commentary).

Bible

Works in this area take as their primary focus the Bible (i.e. Jewish and Christian Scripture), and draw from those texts Biblical views and perspectives on aging.

Other Religions

In this section we have gathered materials which are not from within the Jewish and Christian traditions. Materials here relate to world religions (Buddhism, Hinduism, etc.) and to other religious traditions (Native Americans, primitive religions, Quechua, etc.). A single item deals with cults.

8. Religious Professionals

The materials in this section focus on the religious professional, that is clergy (or clergy-in-training), religious educators, and members of religious communities. There are a variety of topics addressed. One group of materials relates to the training of seminarians and educators for future work with older adults, another to the knowledge of and training about the aging process for already-employed religious professionals. Other topics include retirement (preparation for and life in) and some specific issues relating to women religious.

9. Special Populations

Each item in this section approaches the question of the pastoral response of church and synagogue to elders and their families from the specific perspective of a chosen population. That is to say, some specific group has been studied (usually using social science methodologies) and the results are presented. Examples include second-generation urban Croatians, the widowed, Blacks, Cubans, American Indians, Chicanos, elderly urban Catholic ethnics, rural Blacks.

A specific benefit of this kind of study is its ability to help the reader realize that not everyone is alike and that humans are always profoundly shaped by class, gender, ethnicity, and cohort.

10. Health and Religion

This section gathers articles, usually written from a social science perspective, which try to detail the relationship between health (mental or physical) and religion in the aged. This section may be of less interest to those actually engaged in pastoral response to the aged for two reasons. First, the practitioner knows from experience that there is some sort of interrelation between religion and health; the people of his or her ministry are both well/not well and religious, however unpredictable the relationship might be. Second, the direction of causality is virtually impossible to assess: are people healthy or sick because they are religious or are they religious because they are healthy or sick. The literature (following life, in this regard) is inconclusive; thus it might seem uninteresting to the religious professional or lay person engaged in ministry.

We have included this section, however, to signal a fairly widespread concern of social scientists in the area of religion and aging, and even in the area of the pastoral response to elders.

PASTORAL RESPONSES TO OLDER ADULTS AND THEIR FAMILIES

Church and Synagogue

COMPREHENSIVE GUIDES TO MINISTRY

Books

1. Angerman, J., & Angerman, S. (1990). <u>Older adult ministry: A guide for the presbytery committee</u>. Louisville, KY: Presbyterian Publishing House, 89p.

Written by two Older Adult Ministry Enablers, this manual is designed to help presbyteries initiate ministries with older adults. Guidelines are provided to help the church translate concern into action: creating a committee or task force on older adult ministry, selecting enablers, and involving congregations.

2. Becker, A. H. (1986). <u>Ministry with older persons: A guide for clergy and congregations</u>. Minneapolis, MN: Augsburg, 221p.

This handbook contains basic information on the myths and realities of aging as well as the faith and ethical concerns of the elderly. Practical guidelines for developing an effective ministry include the traditional ministry of word and sacrament, ministry of information and referral, ministry of the ombudsman, and ministry of advocacy.

3. Bergmann, M., & Otte, E. (1981). <u>Engaging the aging in ministry</u>. St. Louis, MO: Concordia, 80p.

This manual is an aid in launching a senior adult ministry geared to individual resources and the condition of the local church. The role of the pastor is to facilitate the development of a program which will be of benefit to seniors and to the whole congregation.

4. Brandt, C. (1978). Forgotten people: Reaching out to the elderly. Chicago, IL: Moody, 127p.

This inspirational text finds the biblical basis for reaching out to the frail and lonely elderly in the example of Jesus who reached out to the downtrodden. Issues raised include responsibilities to the elderly, special needs and characteristics, and how the church can creatively help their elderly.

5. Burns, R. J. (1977). A program for older adults in the church. Grand Rapids, MI: Baker Book House, 69p.

This book asks the questions, "What does it mean to grow old?" and "How can the church meet the needs of senior adults?" It gives creative, practical guidance to local churches and other groups. Part one focuses on the aging process; part two presents the how of church programming.

6. Clingan, D. F. (1980). Aging persons in the community of faith: A guidebook for churches and synagogues on ministry to, for, and with the aging. Indianapolis, IN: Indiana Commission on the Aging and Aged, 82p.

This guidebook, now a classic, assists clergy and lay leaders to organize, plan and create a more effective ministry to, for, and with the aging; to stimulate thinking about program models; to encourage congregational-community teamwork; and to fulfill the mission inherent in the faith they profess.

7. Gray, R. M., & Moberg, D. O. (1977). The church and the older person. Grand Rapids, MI: William B. Eerdmans, 227p.

This is a book on the place, function, and meaning of religion in the lives of older persons, the first to be solidly based on the findings of social science research (interviews). There are also chapters on the church as a resource for older persons, and older persons as resources for the church.

8. Hoyer, H. C. (1978). <u>Aging and the response of faith</u>. New York: Lutheran Church in America, 21p.

This booklet is a guide to the study of the 1978 social Statement of the Lutheran Church in America, adopted by the Ninth Biennial Convention, Chicago, Illinois: "Aging and the Older Adult" appended at the end of the guide.

9. Kadar, R. A. (1974). <u>Senior adult utilization and ministry handbook</u>. Clearwater, FL: Kader Specialties, 32p.

The purpose of this handbook was to motivate churches and organizations to utilize "senior adult manpower" and to minister to the older adults. "The efforts presented in this handbook are down-to-earth, practical and workable because they have been tried through experience" (p. 2).

10. Kerr, H. L. (1980). <u>How to minister to senior adults in your church</u>. Nashville, TN: Broadman, 139p.

Written from the author's background in ministry and service to senior adults, this small book presents information to aid pastors and church leaders in establishing and improving ministry programs with and to senior adults. This book includes a rationale for ministry, strategies for planning for senior ministry, special needs and concerns, and evaluation.

11. Lancaster, H. (1980). <u>Aging</u>. Independnece, MO: Herald, 72p.

This is one of six pamphlets in a series on issues related to the pastoral care function of the Reorganized Church of Jesus Christ of Latter Day Saints. It deals with general information about aging and presents topics for group study and action on needs identification, ministry planning, attitudes about aging, changes and adjustments, mortality, and the meaning of work and retirement.

12. Laurello, B. J. (1979). <u>Ministering to the aging: Every Christian's call</u>. Ramsey, NJ: Paulist Press, 88p.

While this little primer on ministering <u>to</u> the aging is dated in many respects, in other ways it is a reminder that there is more unfinished work to do today than there was in the late 1970's and that some substantial progress has been made in conceptualizing ministry <u>with</u> the aging.

13. Mason, J. M. (1978). <u>The fourth generation</u>. Minneapolis, MN: Augsburg, 168p.

American society has four or even five generations living concurrently. The author recognizes this and writes of the need for church and society to adjust to this structural change in our culture. He pleads for a new awareness, for advocacy, and for concrete responses to the needs and circumstances of this oldest age group.

14. McClellan, R. W. (1977). <u>Claiming a frontier: Ministry and older people</u>. Los Angeles, CA: Ethel Percy Andrus Gerontology Center, University of Southern California, 125p.

This book deals with the relation of church practices to successful aging. It is unique in that it presents the results of a series of experiments that have been field tested and evaluated.

15. <u>Older adult ministry: A resource for program development</u>. (1987). Atlanta, GA: Presbyterian Publishing House, 217p.

This loose-leaf guide for program development is designed to help clergy, Christian educators, and members of committees on older adult ministry develop nurturing ministries by and with older adults. The first three chapters look at biblical and theological, gerontological, and ecclesiastical foundations for older adult ministries. The remaining ten chapters offer specific strategies for successful programs.

16. Osborne, R. (Ed.). (1975). <u>Mission action group guide: The aging</u>. Birmingham, AL: Woman's Missionary Union, 48p.

This resource describes the mission action group, orients members to the needs and opportunities for mission action with older adults, and describes how to conduct surveys, and how to plan, conduct and evaluate mission activities that will help older persons feel useful and of worth.

17. Otterness, O. G., & Mundahl, T. T. (1987). <u>Ministry with older persons</u>. Minneapolis, MN: Augsburg, 64p.

This manual helps local church congregations to plan a ministry to and with older persons. It includes biblical and theological foundations for ministry with older adults; a primer on aging; and a step-by-step planning process, program models, and committee worksheets.

18. Prevost, T. E. (1976). <u>Aging--senior impact: Handbook on aging and senior adult ministries</u>. Atlanta, GA: Home Mission Board, SBC, 40p.

This booklet approaches a whole ministry through the church which includes five areas: spiritual, education, socialization, service, and recreation.

19. Rendahl, J. S. (1984). <u>Working with older adults</u>. Arlington Heights, IL: Harvest, 130p.

Written by an older adult, this manual draws from the first-hand observations and research of its author, the coordinator of senior adult ministries for the board of Christian education, the Baptist General Conference. The focus of the manual is programming for older adults. The style is lively and practical and the manual includes checklists for local congregations and questionnaires and other forms for older adults.

20. Robb, T. B. (1968). <u>The bonus years: Foundations for ministry with older persons</u>. Valley Forge, PA: Judson Press, 156p.

This is one of several early books discussing the nature of ministry with older adults in the local church. While the author does not tell "how to do it," he does present a perceptive study of the scope of the problem, the characteristics of aging, the needs of older persons, and examples of existing programs.

21. Robb, T. B. (1991). <u>Growing up: Pastoral nurture for the later years</u>. New York: Haworth.

This book describes tasks and program suggestions to aid religious professionals assisting older congregants to cope with and overcome barriers limiting their expression of faith in God.

22. Segler, F. M. (1975). <u>Alive! And past 65!: How to deal with aging for families and church leaders</u>. Nashville, TN: Broadman, 126p.

The author is a retired professor of pastoral ministry working as an associate in the area of pastoral care in Broadway Baptist Church. The content and style of the book are inspirational and common-sensical. The author's own investment in the various topics adds flavor to the text.

23. Seltzer, S. (Ed.). (1979). <u>So teach us to number our days: A manual on aging for synagogue use</u>. New York: Union of American Hebrew Congregations, 90p.

This resource for congregational Aging Awareness Committees helps them design informative and effective outreach programs for older adult members and their families. It contains information on aging, organizing an aging awareness program, programs reported by Union of American Hebrew Congregations, and an aging awareness test for congregations.

24. Stafford, V. (1953). <u>Older adults in the church</u>. Nashville, TN: Methodist Publishing House, 96p.

This pioneer program resource is to be used to help adults through the church "become more joyous, meaningful, growing participants in the life of home, church, and community" (p. 4). Subjects include outreach (bringing older adults into the church fellowship), older adults as learners, recreation, older adults serving others, older adults at worship, and effective program planning and administration.

25. Steer, H. P. (1966). <u>Caring for the elderly</u>. London: S.P.C.K., 106p.

Written as part of the S.P.C.K.'s "Library of Pastoral Care," this book covers a wide range of topics: characteristics, restrictions, and opportunities of old age; living conditions; wholeness and holiness; temporal and spiritual care; the minister to the aged. A dominant theme is that only goodness of character really benefits old age.

26. Stubblefield, J. M. (Ed.). (1986). <u>A church ministering to adults: Resources for effective adult Christian education</u>. Nashville, TN: Broadman, 318p.

While this book covers the whole range of adult Christian education, two short chapters by Lucien E. Coleman deal with older adults: "Later Adult Years," (demographics, mythology of aging, problems and promises of retirement) and "Senior Adults: Expanding Opportunities for Ministry/Service" (ministry with older adults, a reservoir of untapped power, guidelines for ministry with older adults).

27. Suseelan, M. A. (Ed.). (n.d.). Resource book on aging. New York: United Church Board for Homeland Ministries, 112p.

This resource book is a response to clergy of the United Church of Christ who wanted to be informed, educated and trained in order to minister to the needs of the aging in their congregations. Part I: Theological Perspectives on Aging; Part II: Description of the Aging; Part III: Services to the Aging; Part IV: Additional Resources on Aging.

28. Taylor, B. E. (1984). The church's ministry with older adults. Nashville, TN: Abingdon Press, 143p.

This handbook for pastors and churches includes suggestions, illustrations, and program ideas designed for clergy and lay people committed to ministry with older adults.

29. Tilberg, C. W. (Ed.). (1980). The fullness of life: Aging and the older adult. New York: Lutheran Church in America, 233p.

This book takes a positive view of the aging process and affirms older persons as those whose dignity is God given. Although not a handbook for planning ministry programs in the church, chapters on psychology of aging, health in the later years, living arrangements, education, community programs, the ministry of the church, and Christian perspectives on aging will benefit individuals as well as committee members planning programs for older adults.

Articles

30. Allen, M. (1987). Gray on gray: Quaker concerns on aging in the United States. In L. Kenworthy (Ed.), Friends face the world (pp. 226-237). Philadelphia, PA: Friends General Conference.

This wide ranging but brief article gives a general overview of Quaker meetings and Friends churches and the aging, including housing and health care for Friends. It then discusses education and the aging, filial obligations, possible family aging programs, and euthanasia and the ethics of aging.

31. Broughton, P. (1988, January). To take seriously older adults. Christian Social Action, 1, 19.

This brief article reports the recommendations of the Task Force on Older Adult Ministries in the United Methodist Church. The task force proposed the establishment of an Advisory/Coordinating Committee on Older Adult Ministries having representatives from general agencies, commissions, jurisdictions, and the Council of Bishops. Responsibilities of this committee are summarized.

32. Glass, J. C. (1990). Religion and aging and the role of education. In R. H. Sherron, & D. Barry Lumsden (Eds.), Introduction to educational gerontology (pp. 109-134). New York: Hemisphere.

This chapter would serve as an excellent guide for establishing older adult programs in churches and synagogues. Glass addresses the responsibility that churches and synagogues have for working with older adults, the religious involvement of the elderly, categories of older adults, objectives of older adult ministry, ways to conceptualize older adult ministry, and the role of education in aging ministry.

33. Hendrickson, M. C. (Ed.). (1986, Summer). The role of the church in aging, Vol. III: Programs and services for seniors. Journal of Religion and Aging, 2(4).

This volume explores a variety of issues related to programs and services for seniors. It includes articles on advocacy, churches as geriatric health care clinics for community-based elders, partnership day-care centers (parish and agency), home sharing, volunteer legal guardianship, congregate housing for frail elderly, retirement homes, church-sponsored long-term care facilities, and the modernization of organization structures for agencies and institutions.

34. Maves, P. B. (1960). Aging, religion, and the church. In C. Tibbitts (Ed.), Handbook of social gerontology: Societal aspects of aging (pp.

698-749). Chicago, IL: University of Chicago.

In this chapter, Maves, a pioneer in the area of religion and aging, presents a detailed study of this topic including an excellent review of the literature to 1960. He explains the sociological factors which complicate any study of religion and aging, presents Judeo-Christian teachings and attitudes relevant to aging, looks at programs for the elderly in the local church, and participation of the elderly in parish programs. The suggestions Maves offers for areas of research are still relevant.

35. Maves, P. B. (Ed.). (1954, September). The church and older people [Special issue]. Pastoral Psychology, 5(46).

The articles in this issue are of more than historical interest. Together they set a standard which was seldom matched in the subsequent 30 years. They are: "Editorial: The Church and Older People" and "The Church in Community Planning," Paul B. Maves; "Some Obstacles in Pastoral Counseling of Older People," J. Lennart Cedarleaf; "Religion and the Aging Process," Seward Hiltner; "'Forsake Me Not'," Orlo Strunk, Jr.; "Old Age and Productive Loss," Martin Gumpert; "Principles of Evangelism According to Christ," Gaines S. Dobbins; "Consultation Clinic: The Minister and the Aged," Paul B. Maves, Martin Gumpert, and C. Ward Crampton.

36. McKay, E. C. (1987, Spring/Summer). Parish ministry and the elderly: Perspectives of pastors and senior parishioners. Journal of Religion & Aging, 3(3/4), 127-137.

This article reports a study of 10 pastors and 72 senior parishioners about the specifically spiritual dimension of programs for seniors. Themes that emerged were seniors as spiritual leaders, stress, the voluntary recluse, non-fragmentation of the parish into age groups, nursing homes, quest for reconciliation, death and dying, need for companionship, and social contact.

37. Moberg, D. O. (1987, May/June). Bibliography on aging for pastors and other church leaders. TSF Bulletin, 17-20.

This is a briefly annotated listing of 43 resources for older adult ministry.

38. United Presbyterian Church, (USA) (1981, July-August). Ministry to and

with aging persons. Church and Society, 71, 29-40.

This article reports the recommendations of the Task Force on Ministries with Aging Persons appointed by the General Assembly Mission Council following the 191st General Assembly in 1979. Strategies for implementing the directions of the 193rd General Assembly dealt with theological education, Christian education, housing, health, long-term care, income security, church employees, and program development.

SPECIFIC PROGRAMS AND MODELS

Books

39. Adams, J. R., & Fletcher, J. C. (1981). Me and my parents, a course for adults. Washington, DC: Alban Institute, 57p.

This 16-session course developed to help adult children explore their relationship with their parents was designed and tested in an Episcopal church. The loose-leaf notebook format allows teachers to adapt the course to the needs of their group and denomination.

40. American Association of Retired Persons. (1989). Grief support training for clergy and congregations: Training manual. Washington, DC: American Association of Retired Persons, 57p.

This training program is designed as a first step in developing long-term grief support systems. It is adaptable to ecumenical/interfaith groups or to single congregations. The three sessions prepare clergy and laypersons to recognize and understand the grief process, as well as to design programs for congregations and communities. All necessary handouts are included.

41. Ammon, G. B. (1972). Adventures with older adults in outdoor settings: A manual of guidance. Philadelphia, PA: United Church, 60p.

This little book assumes is that the church can work with older adults in outdoor settings using an enabling model of ministry. It offers very specific recommendations on organization and planning, outdoor settings for camps and retreats, outdoor programs, outdoor activities, and areas of interest and concern.

42. Baker, P.   (n.d.).   Loving outreach and visitation to the elderly and shut-ins. Bryan, TX: First Presbyterian Church.

A manual for training volunteers in the L.O.V.E.S. program, a visitation program for persons who are homebound or institutionalized. The packet contains a training guide, sample forms, brochure, and two books: Healing with time and love and Ministry of love.

43. Bradford, C. W. (1983). Ministry for retired persons: A simple narrative of the evolvement of a concept. Baton Rouge, LA: The Retired Club, Reily Memorial University United Methodist Church, 123p.

The main purpose of this book is to present the early motives, objectives, leadership, church environment, and structure of the University United Methodist Church Retired Club. The main focus of the club was to provide fun, food, and fellowship for the members. Club members helped with other ministry programs such as providing tapes of worship services to homebound church members.

44. Cook, G. (1978). Mission action: Retirees on mission. Memphis, TN: Brotherhood Commission of the Southern Baptist Convention, 70p.

The author, who started the first Southern Baptist Conference on Aging in 1974, has written this guide to help churches and associations encourage senior adults to discover their ministry gifts and volunteer for missions in their own and the world community. This guide can be used for groups or individuals as each chapter contains a study and discussion guide and a meditation and Bible study.

45. Dimmock, A. E. (1982). Final report to the NRTA-AARP Andrus Foundation on a research project making an evaluation and comparison of six models designed by leaders of local congregations to enhance the spiritual well-being of their older adults. Unpublished manuscript, The Presbyterian School of Christian Education, Center on Aging, Richmond, VA.

This research studied educational models developed and implemented in several congregations in the southern United States (Presbyterian, United Methodist, Episcopal) to determine their effect on the spiritual well-being of members 60 years of age and older. Of the designs in the three groups of models tested, the one most effective in enhancing life satisfaction and spiritual growth as defined in the study was a six-session intergenerational church school class.

46. Doughty, S. V. (1984). Ministry of love: A handbook for visiting the aged. Notre Dame, IN: Ave Maria Press, 93p.

Using anecdotes from his ministerial experience, pertinent information from the medical and counseling professions, and good common sense, the author presents the skills and sensitivities necessary to deal with the confused or disoriented, helping them adjust to a dramatically different and difficult life. Doughty offers practical advice for ongoing visits, suggestions for group programs, aids for prayer and worship, and ways to share God's love.

47. Hynson, D. (Ed.). (1989). Honor your father & mother: For middle adults who love and care for older adults. Nashville, TN: Graded, 112p.

Study sessions consist of seven core sessions: myths and realities; concern and caregiving; the sandwich generation; relating and communicating; responding to sensitivities and needs; our spiritual journey; and maturity in Christ. Six spin-off sessions are also included: ministries by, with, and for older adults; living arrangements; dimensions of retirement; loving again; care for the frail elderly; final arrangements. A separate participant manual is available.

48. Lawson, R. J. (1983). Our congregations's ministries with older adults. Nashville, TN: Discipleship Resources, 84p.

This useful handbook for churches planning older adult ministries presents twenty-five models, grouped under five general headings--worship, study, service, fellowship, and general.   Resources (media, talent bank form, stewardship survey, worship litany, and "The Shepherd's Center" approach) are included in the section on Resources for Ministry.

49. Lewis, M. A. (1989). Religious congregations and the informal supports of the frail elderly: Project summary. New York: Third Age Center, Fordham University, 40p.

This summary of the Interfaith Volunteers Caregivers Program is important for the conclusions and recommendations it makes to churches and synagogues.

50. Rhea, J. I. (1983). <u>When parents grow old: A training design for use with adult children caring for aging parents</u>. Atlanta, GA: Presbyterian Office on Aging.

This six-session training design presents information on the changing lifestyle and behavior of older parents, personal feelings of the adult child, family relationships, dealing with tension and anxiety during times of crisis, and community resources. Questions for discussing the role of the church are dispersed throughout the sessions.

51. Vandenburgh, M. (1975). <u>Fill your days with life</u>. Glendale, CA: Regal Books, 186p.

A description of the Senior Adult program of one evangelical church, this book explores the ministry of the Jolly Sixties, a "mighty army for God" that results "in souls being saved, the elimination of loneliness, and a challenge for service" (p. 2).

Articles

52. Apel, M. D. (1986, Spring). Attitudes and knowledge of church members and pastors related to older adults and retirement. <u>Journal of Religion & Aging</u>, <u>2</u>(3), 31-44.

This study reports that pastors and members had a generally positive view of retirement. Findings indicate, however; 1) a need for learning experiences throughout the lifespan concerning personal adjustment, social relationships, health care, and economic planning; 2) a need for more intergenerational relationships; 3) pre-retirement planning.

53. Breien, P. C. (1986, Spring). "Involving the Elderly in Mission"--A service project. <u>Journal of Religion & Aging</u>, <u>2</u>(3), 77-85.

This article reports a program in a church of 1200 members which augmented inadequate natural social networks with intentionally planned networks. Programming was balanced between traditional and innovative. The effects included strengthening senior networks, increasing integration of seniors and others, and providing a point of entry for those new to the church.

54. Buchen, I. H. (1980, January/February).   An introduction to future scenarios: The issue of the elderly. Church and Society, 70, 41-47.

Using a variety of categories, the author draws a positive scenario on aging in the Presbyterian Church (USA), a mixed scenario, and a negative scenario. Categories of described are religious, economic, political, social, psychological, medical, communal, and education.

55. Custer, C. E. (1988). Preparing lay persons to work with older adults in the local church. Educational Gerontology, 14, 327-341.

This article examines the opportunity facing the church to extend its ministry and mission to older adults within the church and community. The author suggests organizational and equipping models for carrying out a work of ministry for, with, and by older adults. Biblical and theolgical underpinnings are emphasized.

56. Folkman, N. (1989, Spring). Cast me not off in the time of old age. Dialogue: A Journal of Mormon Thought, 22(1), 87-97.

Several true life stories are presented to encourage the Church of Jesus Christ of the Latter-Day Saints to develop programs to meet the needs of the growing numbers of older adult church members.   Assistance for family caregivers--usually women--of these elderly is strongly advocated.

57. Katschke-Jennings, B., & Healy, D. (1987, Spring/Summer). Remarriage and the elderly. Journal of Religion & Aging, 3(3/4), 1-11.

This article identifies the distinctive needs and circumstances of elderly people in remarriage. As many older adults are church related, the clergy need to know who are the elderly and what are their unique needs, what are the issues that surround their decisions to remarry, what constitutes adequate counsel, how this counsel differs from that given younger or middle-aged couples, how to give appropriate sex education, how to relate with adult stepchildren, and ageist attitudes perpetuated by sermons.

58. King, J. C. (1980, October). Firt Southern Presbyterian Church--one look at ministry with aging people. Austin Seminary Bulletin, 96(3), 31-38.

This article outlines the history of First Southern Presbyterian Church's ministry with the elderly in its central-city congregation. The heart of the program is Senior Tuesdays consisting of worship and lunch.

59. Schreck, H. (1991). The urban church: A healing community for the older person. Journal of Religious Gerontology, 7(3), 11-26.

This article reports a successful intentional creation of community for the at-risk older person (Volunteer Chore Ministry). Its success derives in large measure from its dependence on a church base and on its respect for the integrity of the local church and its ministry.

60. Snyder, R. (1981, July). An enterprise of transgenerational adulthood. The Christian Ministry, 12, 5-14.

This article explains the concept of "transgenerational adulthood [as] "becoming members one of another (being membered) in a group composed of people from all four adult eras of growing toward being fully a person" (p. 14). Intergenerational suggests that each generation originated on its own and is a word belonging to "the kingdom of individualism." First Presbyterian Church of San Anselmo, California designed and piloted a transgenerational event consisting of five consecutive Wednesday evenings.

61. Thompson, J. E. (1986, Spring). Life care ministry: The church as part of the elderly support network. Journal of Religion & Aging, 2(3), 65-76.

This article reports how one church hired a full-time staff person to develop and direct a program with the elderly in a congregation where 18% were senior citizens. Life Care Ministries determined specific needs, recruited committed individuals, implemented services and programs, made personal contact, and involved increasing numbers of participants.

62. White, O. Z. (1986, Fall/Winter). Communities within communities. Journal of Religion & Aging, 3(1/2), 193-205.

The author identifies several programs in San Antonio, Texas, which involve a number of the elderly who live in the area in urban or suburban settings. The author predicts that the communities to which the future elderly relate will be more able to meet the needs of individuals in a face-to-face way (communities within communities) because those now reaching retirement age are not unprepared for their new status in the life cycle.

Dissertations

63. Alexander, J. (1989). <u>Developing possibilities for ministry with the aging</u> (Doctor of Ministry thesis, Drew University). <u>DAI</u>, <u>50</u>, 1689A.

This project evaluated the ministry with the aging of the congregation served by the author. Personal contact showed areas to be strengthened or developed. Suggestions include the removal of physical barriers and the implementation of numerous ovations to make the elderly feel important in the life and work of the church.

64. Carl, L. D. (1982/1983). <u>A ministry to adults coping with the aging process in the second half of life</u> (Doctor of Ministry thesis, Drew University). <u>DAI</u>, <u>43</u>, 3023A.

The purpose of this study was to help adults in the second half of life cope with aging through an experimental four-session program (aging as change, attitudes toward aging, aging as loss, aging as fulfillment). The project includes an evaluation of the program's theory, design and leadership.

65. Champion, B. J. (1987). <u>Developing a program of visitation to the elderly in Central United Methodist Church, Canton, North Carolina</u> (Doctor of Ministry thesis, Drew University). <u>DAI</u>, <u>49</u>, 1828A.

This project used a design team to research the needs of elderly congregants. A task force selected from the design team planned a program of pastoral care through lay visitation.

66. Chase, L. W. (1982/1983). <u>Establishing a system for priority use of pastoral time with older church members</u> (Doctor of Ministry thesis, Princeton Theological Seminary). <u>DAI</u>, <u>43</u>, 3024A.

This project evaluated pastoral contacts with older people over a period of eight weeks in order to assess how best the pastor might use the time alloted to pastoral visitation. Criteria are developed which describe creative older people (who need little pastoral care), people struggling toward creative response (where a dynamic relationship might focus their creative energies and help them get on with their lives), and those people who have little or no creative response (and who need a great deal of support, but from whom little can be expected in terms of further growth).

67. Cobban, J. B. (1988/1989). A strategy for changing values relative to the aging population in local churches. (Master of Theology thesis, The Southern Baptist Theological Seminary). Masters Abstracts International, 27, 30.

This thesis offers a model campaign strategy to be used in a congregation to accomplish purposive social change. The theoretical construct is taken from Kohlberg's developmental theory of values.

68. Cook, J. W. (1971). An application of the disengagement theory of aging to older persons in the church (Doctor of Theology dissertation, Boston University School of Theology). DAI, 33, 3011A.

This dissertation studied whether older persons who retire and move to Florida disengage from the church and from expressions of piety more than those who retire and remain in their home community. In the sample studied it was found (among other findings) that moving to a new community speeds the process of disengagement. Disengagement from expressions of piety was more difficult to assess.

69. Forsman, A. R. (1982). Developing a lay ministry of personal care among senior adults at First Covenant Church (Doctor of Ministry thesis, Drew University). DAI, 43, 1489A.

The project was designed to train, in four sessions, a group of lay people for ministry among older adults, in order to reconcile alienated or estranged elders and return them to the mainstream of congregational life.

70. Inman, R. F. (1985). Toward the development of a lay ministry with elderly shut-ins in the local church (Unpublished Doctor of Ministry thesis, Columbia Theological Seminary).

This project is the author's response to the need for a more intensive ministry of pastoral care with the elderly shut-ins of his congregation. He functioned as a pastoral enabler and overseer to train and supervise four laity in a three-month ministry with eight shut-ins.

71. Jones, B. M. (1985). Beautiful autumn: the church's ministry with senior adults (Unpublished Doctor of Ministry thesis, Western Conservative Baptist Seminary).

This project is a training manual for non-professional volunteers who wish to work with senior adults in home, community, or church. It includes a model for a senior adult group and surveys which can be used in communities and institutions.

72. Kees, J. C. (1981). Engaging an older congregation in a program of pastoral care with and for the aging in Pitcairn, Pennsylvania (Doctor of Ministry thesis, Drew University). DAI, 42, 1191A.

Based on an informal survey, this study sought to design a program of pastoral care for the aging in a small town. Pastoral care was understood as offering assurance, companionship, affirmation, solace, service, or referral. The study concluded that there was vitality and creativity as well as need in the older congregants.

73. Lawler, T. J. (1987). Implications of the Gospel of Luke for frail older persons and older persons who are anxious regarding future frailty (Unpublished Doctor of Ministry thesis, San Francisco Theological Seminary).

This project reviews sections of the Gospel of Luke and suggests insights regarding spiritual meanings of the texts to frail older persons and for persons who are anxious about future frailty. The author's insights form part of a basis for a spirituality of aging.

74. Lee, R. W. (1982). Developing a ministry to aged shut-ins aimed at increasing positive self-images (Doctor of Ministry thesis, Drew University). DAI, 43, 1190A.

In this project volunteers were carefully trained, shut-ins were interviewed about their needs and desires, and the process of activities was engaged. Both test results (pre-, post-) and personal observations (of volunteers, nursing home staff, families and friends) indicated positive change, although personal observations revealed a greater change than did the tests.

75. Liebschutz, T. P. (1986). An historical review, evaluation and suggestions for the future of Temple Tifereth Israel's Xtra Years of Zest (XYZ) Club (Unpublished Doctor of Ministry thesis, Boston University School of Theology).

This evaluation of a program in light of the entire synagogue shows that it does not qualify as a model for other congregations to emulate. The project includes a focused, annotated bibliography on contemporary Reform Judaism and aging.

76. Maddin, J. L. (1989). Developing and implementing a ministry with church members who are homebound (Doctor of Ministry thesis, Drew University). DAI, 50, 2115A.

This project studies a special ministry of study, worship, fellowship, and service in the homes of the homebound members of a church. Many of these persons are elderly. The model proposed involves extensive lay participation.

77. Mann, R. C. (1981). A practical guide for older persons and ministry (Doctor of Ministry thesis, Drew University). DAI, 42, 1081A.

This study designed a model for ministry to and with older adults in the local church. The First Baptist Friday Club (FB/FC) grew rapidly and its ministries reached across age barriers, and thus led to the incorporation of a wide range of talents into a common ministry.

78. Mershon, J. M. (1979). Aging, and a model program for older persons in the church (Doctor of Ministry thesis, School of Theology at Claremont). DAI, 40, 1527A.

A study by questionnaire of a 4500 member church (University Church of Seventh Day Adventists, Loma Linda, California) led to the formation of three organizational units to meet expressed needs: social, lifetime learning, and the outreach of serving others in continuing valued self-giving.

79. Nabors, O. R. (1987). Establishing a support group and equipping members of the community and First Christian Church, Richardson, Texas to

relate to aging parents (Unpublished Doctor of Ministry thesis, Brite Divinity School at Texas Christian University).

Four seminars explored with participants how people age and how adult children can cope effectively with parents in relationships altered by aging. Sessions included the aging process, relating to aging parents, caring for aging parents, and available community resources.

80. Rodeheaver, D. (1982). Eastland's elders: Aging and status maintenance in a West Virginia church community (Doctor of Philosophy dissertation, West Virginia University). DAI, 43, 3776B.

This study of a small Methodist church in north-central West Virginia showed that the church community facilitates close friendships among the elders which in turn encourage community involvement. Further, the community provides for continued status of the elders by maintaining their visibility, permitting continued participation and leadership, recognizing past contributions, and emphasizing a shared commitment to the church.

81. Strah, J. C. (1985/1986). Church services wanted by 80 older members of the United Church of Christ (Doctor of Social Work thesis, Fordham University). DAI, 47, 1362A.

This study of 80 members age 65 and older from four congregations indicated that age is not a predictor of a desire for services (spiritual, social/interactional, or concrete). However, lack of physical mobility does make a difference. People who lack physical mobility tend to want more services than do their mobile/independent counterparts.

PROGRAMS FROM PARTICULAR PERSPECTIVES

Books

82. Bier, W. C. (Ed.). Aging: Its challenge to the individual and to society. New York: Fordham University, 292p.

This book was the eighth in the Fordham University Psychology Department's Pastoral Psychology Series which grew out of institutes designed primarily for clergy. The topics presented are still of interest although their presentation seems dated in many regards.

83. Brown, J. P. (1971). <u>Counseling with senior citizens</u>. Philadelphia, PA: Fortress, 144p.

This book emphasizes practical help for the minister/counselor working with seniors. Some topics are problem-centered: health, housing, part-time work and welfare. Some topics emphasize opportunity-centered programs: the role of religion in the aging process, and relating the church program to the needs of seniors. The bibliographies are dated, but of particular use for understanding the development of this field in the 1950's.

84. Faber, H. (1984). <u>Striking sails: A pastoral-psychological view of growing older in our society</u> (K. R. Mitchell, Trans.). Nashville, TN: Abingdon, 158p.

Translated from Dutch, this book is written mainly for people who have a pastoral relationship with older persons. The author identifies shifts in pastoral patterns which create difficult problems for modern pastoral workers. In addition to arriving at a theoretical or more inclusive view of aging, the author describes the world of the aging through observation, empathic thinking, and feeling. He also describes pastoral work with the elderly--specific ways to help as well as specific pastoral dangers (e.g., seeing the old as already dying).

85. Glass, J. C. (1979). <u>Growing through adulthood: Can the church help?</u> Nashville, TN: Discipleship Resources, 14p.

An overview of adult development designed to help persons in local churches understand some of the changes which occur in adults as they progress through the life span. Developmental theories discussed include Erikson, Feibleman, Sheehy, Levinson, Vaillant, and Gould.

86. Morgan, J. H. (Ed.). (1976). <u>Ministering to the elderly: Perspectives and opportunities</u>. Wichita, KS: Kansas Newman College, 48p.

The Institute on Ministry and the Elderly printed these three lectures presented at Kansas Newman College at its 1976 Annual Symposium. "The Older American; Social Psychological Needs," by Helena Znaniecki Lopata reveals that not only do most older women live alone, but few older women mention receiving help from rabbis, priests, ministers or church members. "Ministering to the Elderly; Needs, Perspectives, and Opportunities," by William Oglesby, Jr. emphasizes the supportive role of the church and pastor. Robert D.

Wheelock, "The Church's Response to the Elderly; Strategies and Opportunities" presents suggestions for lay Christians concerned with ministry programs for older adults.

Articles

87. Becker, A. H. (1979, Spring). Judgment and grace in the aging process. Pastoral Pscyhology, 27(3), 181-190.

The experience of sin and judgment in old age often involves self-recrimination, sometimes reinforced by culture or family. The sins of the elderly, often more of attitudes than actions, can bring an acute sense of unworthiness. Attitudes may include stagnation, narcissism, despair, unfaith, un-trust. Guilt, which includes a longing for love and a fear or dread of rejection, may lead the elderly into self-atoning mechanisms. "This process generates the almost frantic need to 'win brownie points' before people and before God" (p. 185). The elderly should be approached with God's law as a basis for reality testing about the aging process and the nature of guilt before God. The pastoral relationship should help the elderly remember the past loving unconditional acceptance of others and bring this into the present.

88. Brink, T. L. (1977, December). Pastoral care for the aged: A practical guide. The Journal of Pastoral Care, 31, 264-272.

The author identifies three potential dangers to mental health in old age: chronic physical conditions, retirement, and changing family relationships. These may result in a variety of psychological manifestations: rigidity, hypochondria, paranoia, depression, and institutional neurosis. The author presents an eight-step plan which the pastoral counselor can use in geriatric cases, in order to bring to bear religion's positive force for mental health in old age.

89. Bryant, M. D. (1989). Re-orienting pastoral care with aging persons. Journal of Religion & Aging, 5(3), 1-16.

The author recommends a shift in pastoral care from caring for to caring with older persons. Specifically he recommends 1) that both an activity theory of aging and a disengagement theory be presupposed, 2) that aging be viewed as a dynamic in lifespan development, 3) that holistic religion is basic to caring, and 4) that theory is important for church programming and organization.

90. Butler, C. (1968). Pastoral needs of older persons: A clinical approach. Journal of Pastoral Care, 22(2), 75-81.

A case-study of a couple in which the man has just retired, this article inquires about appropriate pastoral care. It assumes a disengagement theory of retirement and is of most interest as an historical snapshot of common pastoral wisdom in 1968.

91. Carstensen, R. N. (1983, Fall). Do we need a theology or hermeneutic of aging? Generations, 8, 31-34.

This article discusses the relation of a theology and hermeneutics of aging. Both present life as a totality, offer dignity and service to the elderly, and teach the spiritual values attainable by the religious discipline throughout life and aging.

92. Cluff, C. B. (1984, August). Pastoral enlightenment for seniors: Do they need it? Do they want it? Journal of the American Geriatrics Society, 32, 609-613.

This article discusses the spirituality (a creative and dynamic process of clarification of life's meaning and the quest for God) and pastoral care of the aged to determine if a pastoral response is needed or wanted. Cluff concludes that if pastoral care is merely a means to impose dogma or doctrine, or tries simply to "fix" pain and loss, then it is neither needed nor wanted. True and necessary pastoral care offers the elderly the space and freedom to seek for God and for life's meaning. Any pastoral "response that fails to acknowledge and embrace this reality fails to address the essence of spiritual need" (p. 612).

93. Creen, E., & Simmons, H. (1977, December). Toward an understanding of religious needs in aging persons. The Journal of Pastoral Care, 31(4), 273-278.

According to the authors, the most crucial religious needs of the aging person are the need for affirmation in the face of death and the need to deal with life as a totality. "These needs occur in the inner, subjective life and if successfully met provide meaning and assist growth as the aging person prepares to face death. Christian faith has a more important role in serving these needs than present Church practice would indicate" (p. 273).

94. Donovan, H. (1956). Pastoral needs of older women. The Journal of Pastoral Care, 10, 170-176.

The author stresses the value of letting older persons speak about old age from within their own experience of it. He notes that "one of the greatest single blocks to creative relationships of older with younger persons is the attitude of younger persons toward old age" (p. 175).

95. Fitchett, G. A. (1983, Spring). Old age and the church: A gift and a challenge. Reformed Review, 36, 109-129.

The author discusses the need for clarity in our own perspectives on age and reviews facts and theories on aging as well as key Bible teachings about this part of life. He then discusses vocation, death, and the use of riches as three areas in which the church should be working with the elderly. He concludes with a section on older persons and the building of the Kingdom.

96. Ford, S. R. (1981, Spring). The social process of aging: Its implications for pastoral ministry. Pastoral Psychology, 29(3), 203-215.

Aging is both a biological and social process. American culture is infatuated with youth and terrified of death. It finds the "typical" traits of the old as undesirable, relegates the old to an "out-group" status, and attempts to manage them, in part, by forcing them to conform to a self-abasing elderly role. To the extent that pastors stereotype the old and develop culturally appropriate methods for dealing with older persons they will concentrate on basic needs of food, shelter, and clothing. Ministry to the person through a genuinely human relationship is based on an awareness of old age as an integral part of human life.

97. Kaye, L. W., & Monk, A. (1987, Fall). Changing views of the function of the contemporary synagogue and the role of the older congregant. The Journal of Aging and Judaism, 2, 3-18.

This article reports a study of full-time students of religious education and graduate counterparts in the synagogue. Students were confident of the capacity of the synagogue to provide a range of programs for the aged. Graduates were more cautious in the sponsorship of clinically-supportive interventions. Students also showed more confidence in the aged fulfilling active leadership roles in the life of the synagogue.

98. Keith, P. M. (1977). Perceptions of needs of the aged by ministers and the elderly. Review of Religious Research, 18(3), 278-282.

Ministers and older adults were questioned about perceived needs for future allocation of resources. There was relative agreement between ministers and elderly on eight services included in the first ten selected by each group: (e.g., legal aid, visitation programs, transportation, homemaker health aids, handyman services, telephone reassurance). By contrast, among the most discrepant rankings are those attached to church membership with older persons. Among services on which ministers and the elderly disagree are services assigned higher ratings by the ministers which would not extend the time a person could live independently. The list of 23 items is included in the report.

99. Moberg, D. O. (1972, January). Religion and the aging family. The Family Coordinator, 47-60.

Moberg reviews literature which indicates that while older adults tend to reduce the amount of external church practices in which they engage, they seem to increase the amount of internal religious attitudes and feelings. While problems with health and transportation may keep the elderly from attending church, ministers who focus their attention on ministries with adolescents and young families appear to contribute to attitudes among the elderly that their presence in church is not wanted. Moberg reminds us all that "religious faith and practice have no age limits" (p. 57).

100. Payne, B. (1988). Religious patterns and participation of older adults: A sociological perspective. Educational Gerontology, 14, 255-267.

The author examines patterns of religious behavior and participation of older adults from sociological perspectives and concludes that the established churches and synagogues will be an increasing source of support for older adults, older adults will be recognized as new resources for the congregation, and their increased number, proportionally, will impact the programs and social structure of congregations.

101. Scudder, D. L. (1958). Organized Religion and the Older Person: A Report on the Eighth Annual Southern Conference on Gerontology. Gainsville, FL: University of Florida.

Papers addressed the tasks of religion in dealing with older persons (Seward Hiltner, Milton Barron, Henry Schumacher), presented research reports and definitions of religion in terms of organizational participation, noted research difficulties, and offered illustrations of the ministry of organized religion to the aged.

102. Simmons, H. C. (1989). Aging. In B. Marthaler (Ed.), New Catholic Encyclopedia (Supplement 1978-1988) (pp. 3-4). Washington, DC: Catholic University of America.

This article deals with the popular understanding of aging in America, the origins of this view, and the Church's ministry to the aging. The cultural view of aging is identified as "active disesteem" (the old are useless, unproductive, and unable to adapt). The church's ministry is seen within a framework of social and theological critique of the cultural status quo.

103. Simmons, H. C. (1989, October). Ministry with older adults: Neither known nor esteemed. Professional Approaches for Christian Educators, 13-16.

This first of four articles analyzes the cultural context in which ministry with older adults occurs, noting that pervasive negative attitudes affect all concerned in this ministry. The article describes a view of old age which is simply an extension of a successful middle age, describes old age as a time of loss (the dominant attitude of mass American culture), and looks at variables (class, ethnicity, gender, and birth cohort) which give shape to the individual experience of old age.

104. Smith, B. K. (1980, October). Letter to a new pastor. Austin Seminary Bulletin, 96(3), 5-14.

This letter asks recent seminary graduates to consider aging in self and others in order to help congregates to learn to live in an "I-Thou" relationship with persons of all ages.

105. Strunk, O. (1954, September). "Forsake me not". Pastoral Psychology, 5, 33-36.

The minister has special responsibilities to add healthy life to later years. This requires an understanding of the psychology of old age. Old people should be included in church programs (although this may contravene the common wisdom that what is needed is "young blood"). The author concedes that "the happiest years of one's life are not the years past fifty, contrary to the 'whistling in the dark' theory that life really begins at seventy" (p. 35). He encourages the minister not to attempt superficial cure-all approaches.

106. Underwood, R. L. (1980, October).   Pastoral care with the elderly. Austin Seminary Bulletin, 96(3), 15-22.

In this essay, the author suggests that reflection on the Scripture and Christian tradition can stimulate creative ways to do pastoral care with the elderly. The covenant image of love for God and neighbor "suggests themes that help clarify the significance of pastoral care competencies such as the creative use of pastoral acts, personal respect, listening, and concreteness" (p. 21).

107. Watkins, D. R. (1989). The graying of America: Do the churches know? Southwestern Journal of Theology, 31, 5-11.

The author addresses church programming in a greying society from the perspective of church growth: discover the needs of persons in the community (spiritual, emotional/mental, relational), develop services which speak to those needs, provide personnel and resources for those services, and make people aware of the availability of services.

108. Willits, F. K., & Funk, R. B. (1989). Prior college experience and attitude change during the middle years: A panel study. International Journal of Aging and Human Development, 29, 283-300.

This study of women and men in midlife (at about age 40 and then 13 years later) showed a positive correlation between prior college attendance and less traditional conceptions of gender-roles and belief about God, and lower feelings of anomie at midlife. This study may have implications for changes of attitudes in old age.

Dissertations

109. Lyman, G. D. (1986). Ministry to the older person through the adaptive task of satisfaction of needs (Unpublished Doctor of Ministry thesis, San Francisco Theological Seminary).

This doctoral ministry project developed guidelines for a ministry which would assist older persons in the process of discovering and engaging in new interest, activities, and relationships as needed as adequate substitutes for the satisfaction of needs.

110. Mendenhall, C. M. (1981). Time and success in the aging process: A process gerontological exploration and its implications for pastoral care of aging persons (Doctor of Philosophy dissertation, School of Theology at Claremont). DAI, 42, 1198A.

The purpose of this study was to construct a general model of successsful aging based on a comprehensive integration of empirical data and metaphysical reflection about aging, and thus to assist in pastoral care and counseling with the aging. The method of study consisted of an inquiry into the dynamics of time and value in aging from social psychological research and from a process metaphysical ontology of human aging.

111. Strong, G. W. (1986). Pastoral care among the very elderly (Doctor of Ministry thesis, Hartford Seminary). DAI, 47, 3531A.
This project reports data gathered over the years on the self-declared spiritual needs of 250 parishioners over 80 years of age. The research method was active listening and observation. An extensive bibliography is included.

112. Thompson, L. G. (1988). The church in transition: An aging church in an aging America (Doctor of Ministry thesis, Fuller Theological Seminary). DAI, 49, 2689A.

This project notes that there is, with the aging of the nation, a continuous supply of senior citizens. The church can develop a plan that has appeal to the elderly and provides an appealing and attractive environment for them. With this approach church growth is likely.

113. White, L. W. (1986). The impact of aging upon the attitudes older church members have about their congregations (Unpublished Doctor of Ministry thesis, Western Theological Seminary).

This project used a research method of convenience sampling with a 103-item questionnaire with a population of 451 active Roman Catholics and Protestants 55 years of age and older. Factor analysis showed five dimensions of religiousity: orthodoxy, personal faith, treatment, satisfaction with life, and dissatisfaction with life. Comparison and correlation of factors and items found a positive attitude about life and about congregations. Findings include: men more than women want to feel useful to their congregations, and recent retirement more than other losses negatively influences attitudes.

WORSHIP, RITUAL, PREACHING, AND HYMNS

Books

114. Fine, I. (1988). <u>Midlife, a rite of passage/The wise woman, a celebration</u>. San Diego, CA: Woman's Institute for Continuing Jewish Education, 44p.

This small volume contains two books. The first presents a model for the celebration of midlife adaptable for Jews and non-Jews including the complete text of a midlife ceremony by Bonnie Feinman. The second book discusses the early history of the wise woman, psychological and social aspects of aging, and gives excerpts from several modern day "Wise Woman Ceremonies".

115. Hymn Society of America. (1976). <u>10 New hymns on aging and the later years</u>. Springfield, OH: Author, 13p.

These 10 hymn texts were selected from over 1200 entries submitted in 1975 to the Hymn Society of America as representing new hymns celebrating the later years of life. Suggested tunes are indicated for each hymn text.

116. <u>Hymns of grace and glory</u>. (1976). Nashville, TN: Abingdon, 106p.

This is a collection of 106 all-time favorite hymns with music, set in extra large type. It includes a topical index, index of tune names, and index of first lines and common titles.

117. Milton, J. M. (1988). <u>Let us worship God together: A liturgy for the nursing home congregation</u> (leader's guide). San Rafael, CA: Ecumenical Convalescent Hospital Ministry of Marin, 21p.

This book developed from the author's experience with conducting weekly ecumenical worship services in nursing homes. It answers questions and provides guidelines for setting up a team approach to nursing home ministry, creating a worship environment in an institutional setting, and an explanation of each section of the worship service. Sample pages to help the residents participate in worship are included.

118. Schirmer, M. A. (1989). Prayer services for the elderly: A manual for ministers to the elderly. Kansas City, KS: Archdioceasan Office for the Aging, 102p.

This manual is intended for parish ministers who conduct prayer services for the ill and the aging. Contents printed in large type include a prayer service for each month of the year, the celebration of a birthday, the memorial of a death, family reunions, Grandparents' Day, retirement, and Senior Citizens' month.

119. Troll, L. E. (Ed.). (1988, July/August). Rituals and reunions [Special issue]. American Behavioral Scientist, 31(6).

This entire issue focuses on rituals and reunions practiced by families (although not necessarily restricted to families) particularly in later life. Articles include "Rituals and Reunions" by Lillian E. Troll, "The Ritualization of Family Ties" by David Cheal, "Reunions" by Mildred M. Seltzer, "Reunions Between Elderly Parents and Their Distant Children" by Mirian S. Moss and Sidney Z. Moss, "Generational Transmission of Family Ritual" by Carolyn J. Rosenthal and Victor W. Marshall, "Socially Controlled Civility" by Colleen Leahy Johnson, and "Etiquette and Ritual in Family Conversation" by Corrine N. Nyedegger and Linda S. Mitteness. The range of articles and specificity of topics suggest this as an important resource for participatory (public) rituals.

Articles

120. Hinrichs, H. J. (1986, Fall/Winter). Intergenerational living and worship: The caring community. Journal of Religion & Aging, 3(1/2), 181-192.

This article reports the Caring Community Project. Congregations are trained to form intentional, intergenerational communities through the discipline of the liturgy. Integrating life and faith in the liturgy within intergenerational communities addresses many issues for the church in ministry with older adults.

Barriers to the practice of Caring Community include the impact of theological training and institutional preoccupation.

121. Mohring, M. J. (1981, December 11). Convalescent homes: Places for ministry. Christianity Today, 25, 70.

This article describes how a church can provide nondenominational worship services in convalescent homes where many of the elderly no longer have ties to a particular church. For ministry teams, the most important parts of the service are the music (20 to 30 minutes at the beginning) and individual prayers at the end. Touching each patient also helps reassure them that God and others care for them.

122. Myerhoff, B. (1984). Rites and signs of ripening: The intertwining of ritual, time, and growing older. In D. I. Kertzer, & J. Keith, Age and anthropological theory (pp. 305-330). Ithaca, NY: Cornell University.

In this excellent essay Myerhoff explains the importance and necessity of ritual in old age. She discusses rites of passage; rituals as cultural performance; memory, re-membering, and reminiscence. "Rituals do not change the hard realities of aging. But if people lived by hard realities only, there would be no need for rituals and symbolic forms. The power of ritual is to change our experience of the world and its worth" (p. 328).

123. Robb, T. B. (1991). Liturgical rites of passage for the later years. Journal of Religious Gerontology, 7(3), 1-9.

The author explores the nature of rites of passage, namely that they help redefine self-understanding and community behavior at times of transition. He reflects on existing liturgical rites and the need for new rites for such life stages as the empty nest, retirement, and final infirmity.

124. Simmons, H. C. (1991, November). "Babette's Feast": Transforming rituals in old age. Liturgy, 9(4).

This article uses a construct of eight questions related to a core value system to ask what is the gift the old have to offer and what is the particular burden they bear, in order to consider appropriate communal rituals of transformation. The questions are what is the relationship between humans and the superhuman, between humans and nature, between humans and other humans, what is the conception of time and space, what is the nature of labor, how shall power be used and why, what is the character of innate human nature, and finally what is the nature of reality.

125. Simmons, H. C. (1990, January). Ministry with older adults: Rites and signs of ripening. Professional Approaches for Christian Educators, 83-86.

This third article in a series on ministry with older adults notes a widespread silence in worship about the concerns of older adults. It recommends deliberate action in liturgy to include the losses and gains of the old, and thus to signal our common humanity with them. Specific rituals are suggested including rituals of a blessed and abundant life, rituals for a long-time member of a congregation who is leaving, and rituals which, in owning the possibility of sin in the old, recognize the possibility of grace.

126. Simmons, H. C. (1990). Countering cultural metaphors of aging. Journal of Religious Gerontology, 7(1/2), 153-166.

This article examines three clusters of metaphors which marginalize older adults: age as physical decline, as aesthetic distance from youth, and age as failure in productivity. Two ways of countering these cultural images are the formation of face-to-face groups of older adults and the creation of rituals in worship which publicly name the realities and experiences of growing old.

127. Smith, W. S. (1989, October). Hymns related to aging. The Hymn, 40, 28-30.

This brief article relates the results of a search for hymns that deal with themes of aging and old age. The article should be of great help in the preparation of age-specific or age-inclusive liturgies and devotions.

128. Westerhoff, J. H., & Willimon, W. H. (1980). Retirement. In J. H. Westerhoff, & W. H. Willimon, Liturgy and learning through the life cycle (pp. 149-152). New York: Seabury.

The authors, seminary teachers of worship and education (Episcopal and United Methodist respectively), propose a ritual for retirement. A declaration of purpose states that the person is now freed from his or her job to begin a new ministry. A time of remembrance looks back at the job which is ending. A proclamation in scripture and homily celebrates life lived and encourages a fresh start. There is a response by the retiring person or family and friends. Finally there is a blessing and sending forth. In order for this ritual to be effective, a time of catechesis is needed to help people prepare for the changes in their lives.

129. Willimon, W. H. (1983, March). Aging and changing in the church. The Christian Ministry, 14(2), 5-6.

In this article the author, a United Methodist pastor, encourages other pastors to learn about the aging process in order to understand the major changes, losses, and challenges faced by older members of their congregations. In doing so, ministers may gain insight into the reasons many older members resist changes and innovations in worship services as well as how to address the reality of aging in liturgy.

Dissertations

130. Doyle, J. A. (1985). The Catholic Rite of Anointing and aging in the Post-Vatican II experimental period (Doctor of Philosophy dissertation, University of Southern California). DAI, 46, 1239A.

This study supported the new Catholic Rite of Anointing and recommended its continuation beyond the period of experimentation.

131. Hinson, R. M. (1983). A methodology for Christian preaching on aging (Doctor of Philosophy dissertation, The Southern Baptist Theological Seminary). DAI, 44, 3403A.

This dissertation explored the Good News as it applies to the elderly and sought to establish criteria for effective Christian preaching on aging. Suggestions were made for improving the environment of preaching, for increasing the likelihood that the sermon speaks to the legitimate concerns of the aged, and for addressing ongoing needs related to everyone's aging.

132. Moore, M. D. (1983). Old People's Day: Drama, celebration, and aging (Doctor of Philosophy dissertation, University of California, Los Angeles). DAI, 44, 249A.

Moore studied studied an annual, indigenous American Festival produced by a small community in the hills of northwestern Arkansas. The celebration has a strong fundamentalist bent, and features hymn singing, testifying, and Holy Spirit-led extemporaneous preaching--all dedicated to honoring the community's elderly. It serves to define the community and to promote fellowship among young and old.   The dissertation also comments on the significance of dramatization for a wide variety of festivals and festive gatherings.

133. Perry, P. J. (1980). A comparative analysis of the treatment of the death theme in children's and adolescent literature pre and post 1970 (Doctor of Education dissertation, University of Colorado at Boulder). DAI, 41, 1378A.

One finding may be of interest in the context of this bibliography, although its interpretation is not self-evident: there has been in post 1970 fiction a substantial increase in the mention or portrayal of religious rites.

EDUCATIONAL PROGRAMS FOR AWARENESS AND ENRICHMENT

Books

134. Aerie, J. (1984-85).   Biblical perspectives on aging. In New ventures in Bible study. Crawfordsville, IN: Geneva Press.

This series of Bible discussions focuses on the biblical and theological aspects of aging.

135. Cheavens, A. D.   (1977).   It's OK to be yourself, senior adult. Nashville, TN: Convention.

This church study course book in large print is for senior adults, ages 60 and above.

136. Dobbins, G. S. (1959). The years ahead. Nashville, TN: Convention, 144p.

This book was written for adults as part of The Church Study Course for Teaching and Training by the Baptist Sunday School Board. Church members could earn credit and diplomas for completing these study courses either in class or home study. This course contains eight chapters with an outline, and suggestions for classwork, discussion and additional reading. The course is designed for ten, 45-minute class periods. Chapters address topics such as the aging process, the use of leisure time, fellowship needs, and serving the church. "The message of the Bible may be the same in words, but it is different in interpretation and application with each changing phase of life. Not to realize this is to run the risk of coming to the end of life on the road that leads to disappointment and failure" (p. 36). Although written in 1959, much of the material could be used today.

137. Episcopal Society for Ministry on Aging. (1985). Affirmative aging: A resource for ministry. Minneapolis, MN: Winston, 178p.

This focussed collection of articles affirms various aspects of aging: aging as a spiritual journey, intergenerational relationships, ministry opportunities, and aging alternatives.   The authors see aging as a human phenomenon and challenge rather than as a series of unfortunate ills and inevitable losses.   In many regards, this book of essays marks a new emphasis in religion and aging. A study guide is available.

138. Griggs, D., & Griggs, P.   (1976).   Generations learning together: Learning activities for intergenerational groups in the church. Livermore, CA: Griggs Educational Service, 139p.

The four parts of this book are: basic concerns, formation of Christian self-identity, learning activities for generations learning together, and additional activities and resources.   The orientation is primarily child-adult, although much could be adapted to include adults of a variety of ages.

139. Gulledge, J.   (1979).   Hooray for grandparents!   Nashville, TN: Convention, 49p.

Developed as a text in The Christian Family of the Church Study Course of the Baptist Sunday School Board, this book contains four chapters on how to become the grandparent you would like to be: Stifling the Stereotypes, Establishing an Endless Rendezvous, Nurturing a Healthy and Happy Relationship, Leaving Behind a Museum of Memories.

140. Harder, B. (Ed.). (1986). <u>Young or old or in between: An</u> <u>intergenerational study on aging</u>. Newton, KS: Faith and Life, 84p.

Written from the Mennonite tradition, this five-session intergenerational study about older adults and the experiences of aging is designed to be used for corporate study in the church. Sessions focus on understanding older adults, retirement, wellness, a person's worth, and growing in the faith. There are two manuals: a participant reader and a leader's guide.

141. Harder, B., & Kropf, M. (1982). <u>Intergenerational learning in the</u> <u>church</u>. Newton, KS: Faith and Life, 81p.

The authors set out a philosophy of intergenerational education and a series of guidelines for implementing intergenerational learning. Three models are then presented in detail: Twelve Becoming, Peace Be With You, and The Bible.

142. Johnson, C. (Ed.). (1981). <u>The second half: A resource to help you</u> <u>prepare for a healthy, happy, secure, and productive old age</u>. Chicago: Covenant, 48p.

These twelve Bible-based lessons have been designed to prepare middle-aged adults for the "afternoon of life." In addition to exploring the problems and potentials of aging from a Christian perspective, it is hoped that these lessons will open up discussion between middle-aged adults and older adults. The lessons include a leader's guide and a participant manual.

143. Koehler, G. E. (1977). <u>Learning together: A guide for intergenerational</u> <u>education in the church</u>. Nashville, TN: Discipleship Resources, 95p.

This book recommends that intergenerational programs include three or more of the following groups: children, youth, young adults, middle adults, older adults. The book is set out as a guide; readers are invited to begin at any point of need.

144. Kortrey, B. (Ed.). (1981). <u>Together: A guide for leaders of</u> <u>intergenerational events</u>. Philadelphia, PA: Fortress, 64p.

This book offers brief but precise guidelines for intergenerational experiences. Eight events for intergenerational groups are then presented. Each event includes Bible content, background information for the leader, event activities, and worship suggestions.

145. McGinnis, J.   (1989).   Helping families care: Practical ideas for intergenerational programs. Bloomington, IN: Meyer-Stone, 153p.

The focus of this book is the fostering of peace and justice through intergenerational learning and sharing. Specific guidelines and programs are presented. A series of worksheets are offered for direct use or as models.

146. Parker, P. L. (Ed.). (1974). Understanding aging. Philadelphia, PA: United Church, 47p.

A resource for use with ten- to fourteen-year-olds, this brief text gives clear directions for its use at various ages and identifies books and additional resources. The programatic core includes four sections: what is old?; how did we get that idea of old?; growing old brings problems; celebration of past and present. Of note is the identification of the role of government in the solution of problems (transportation, housing, medical bills, money for food).

147. Reichert, S., & Reichert, R. (1976). In wisdom and the spirit: A religious education program for those over sixty-five. New York: Paulist, 87p.

The purpose of this book is to provide continuing education for Christians in the church. The program is based on three presuppositions: 1) that the necessary physical and psychic needs of the elderly have been met, 2) that older persons have the capacity for growth and service, 3) that older persons who are nearing the end of their life need to understand what eternal life implies. The program consists of five units: the phenomenon of aging; the priesthood of the elderly; prayer and spiritual life; reconciliation and Eucharist; and death, dying and resurrection.

148. Schirmer, M. A. (Ed.). (1983). Understanding and appreciating the aging: A handbook for elementary teachers. Kansas City, KS: Catholic Church Office for Services to the Aging, Archdiocese of Kansas City.

This is a handbook of curriculum units for teachers of grades kindergarten through eight to introduce awareness of the aging process. Each unit presents concepts designed for developing personal growth and self-understanding, recognition of the gifts of older adults as well as their needs and rights, and service and action within the social contexts.   The units are basically ecumenical and can be used in religious education classes, regular classrooms, Bible schools, and integrated into other classes (e.g., social studies).   Also included are prayer services, a bibliography for teachers, information sources, and AV materials.

149. Schirmer, M. A. (Ed.). (1984). Understanding and appreciating the aging: A handbook for secondary teachers.   Kansas City, KS: Catholic Church Office for Services to the Aging, Archdiocese of Kansas City.

This is a handbook of curriculum units for teachers of grades nine through twelve to introduce awareness of the aging process, the gifts older adults have to offer, and knowledge of their rights and needs.   Like the elementary curriculum, each unit is basically ecumenical and can be used in religious education classes and regular classes.   Prayer services, a bibliography for teachers, information sources, and AV materials are included.

150. Turnage, M. N., & Turnage, A. S. (1984). Graceful aging: Biblical perspectives.   Atlanta, GA: Presbyterian Office on Aging, 45p.

This is a collection of correspondence between three surviving spouses of three couples who had been close friends.   The letters helped these three deal with aging and to share insights about Bible passages which posed problems and possibilities.   Exercises and questions are included for adults using the letters as a starting place for group study on the Bible and aging.

151. Unitarian Universalist Association.   (1975).   Aging and awareness. Boston, MA: Author, 73p.

This kit enhances awareness and raises consciousness regarding the universality of aging, its processes, and its problems.

152. Vogel, L. J.   (1984).   The religious education of older adults. Birmingham, AL: Religious Education, 217p.

This book is written for religious educators, pastors, and others who plan and implement religious education programs for older adults, and for older adults themselves. Topics focus on: how older adults learn; the history of older adult education; the author's model for religious education with older adults; teaching older adults; religious education planning and implementation for older adults.

153. Vogel, L. J. (1989). <u>Teaching older adults</u>. Nashville, TN: Discipleship Resources, 48p.

A guide to help teachers in the church to engage in educational ministry with, by, and for older adults. Contains inspirational and practical ideas for planning teaching and learning experiences with older adults.

154. White, J. W. (1988). <u>Intergenerational religious education: Models, theory, and perscription for interage life and learning in the faith community</u>. Birmingham, AL: Religious Education, 290p.

In this comprehensive examination of intergenerational religious education, the author presents his tested model for successful intergenerational religious education along with models being used in several parishes. Theory and research are supplemented by concrete suggestions on building and maintaining intergenerational programs.

Articles

155. Glass, J. C., & Scott, V. C. (1989). Educational preferences of older adults and implications for local congregations. <u>Journal of Religion & Aging</u>, <u>5</u>(3), 43-58.

This research project studied older adults in 22 churches in North Carolina to determine their preferences for either "instrumental" activities (those with goals outside and beyond the act of education) or "expressive" activities (those which have their goal in the act of learning itself). Persons with preference for instrumental learning experiences, persons with higher levels of education and white collar workers opted for expressive learning experiences.

156. Graendorf, W. C. (1983). Biblical principles for ministering to older adults. <u>Christian Education Journal</u>, <u>4</u>(1), 38-45.

Written from an Evangelical Christian perspective, this article presents five foundational principles based on scripture for developing an educational ministry for older adults: the older adult as a person of value, an object of love, a person with resources, a person with a future, and a useful disciple.

157. Kasakove, D. P. (1989, Summer). A look at films and videotapes on Judaism and aging. The Journal of Aging and Judaism, 3, 187-190.

The author reviews the videos "Grandma Didn't Wave Back," and "Young at Heart" in detail, and mentions "The Miracle of Intervale Avenue," "Sparks Among the Ashes," "A Conversation with George Burns," and "A Conversation with Rabbi Robert Schur.".

158. Levine, C. (1989, Fall). Resources for teaching about the aged. The Journal of Aging and Judaism, 4, 7-20.

This article gives a detailed review of resources (primarily printed and typewritten) for teaching about the aged. "Why Be Good," "The Aged in Jewish Tradition Study Guide," "Aging and Judaism," "An All-School Unit on Aging," "Bridging Generations: A Seventh Grade Life Cycle Unit Focusing on Identifying Perceptions and Realities as We Relate to the Elderly in Our Society," "Come Grow Old With Me: Aging in Judaism is a Lifelong Process," "From Generation to Generation to Generation: An Experiential Approach to the Teaching of the Elderly in our Community," "Gemilut Hasadim Unity, The Aged, Intermediate Level," "Growing Older," (Keeping Posted, Vol. 27), "Honoring the Elderly," "Jewish Attitudes Towards the Aged," "The Jewish Elderly: An Integrated Teaching Unit for the Jewish Day School," "Jewish Ethics and the Aged," "Living and Learning with the Aged," "Miracle at Intervale: Jewish Survival in the South Bronx" (slide/tape), "Teaching Elementary and Middle School Students about the Aged: A Judaic, Historical Perspective," and "The Tree of Life".

159. Lipco, L., & Katz, J. (1989). A practical guide to resources for the synagogue. The Journal of Aging and Judaism, 3, 128-132.

The authors present a brief resource guide including issues a needs assessment committee will have to consider, a Gerontology Resource Center for the synagogue library, and appropriate programming.

160. Lippmann, E. (1989, Fall). The ocean, daily life, and Jewish thinking. The Journal of Aging and Judaism, 4, 45-52.

This article presents a complete instructional design for small group study with older adults ages 70 to 90. The ocean is selected as the topic because it is a commonplace experience for many elderly Jews. It is hoped that this study will serve as a model on how to connect everyday life with Jewish thinking.

161. Ng, D. (1980). The church's educational ministry with the aging. Austin Seminary Bulletin, 96(3), 23-30.

This essay builds a rationale for educational ministry with the aging from the wisdom of Erikson (sense of integrity), Butler (life review), and Sherrill (working toward simplification).

162. Simmons, H. C. (1991, Spring). Religious instruction about aging and old age: What the journals are saying. The Living Light, 27, 254-263.

This article inquires about the specific content of religious instruction about aging and old age: i.e. what precise themes, concerns, motifs characterize writing about religion and aging in the recent past. The principal set of writings analyzed are the 102 items listed under "Religion" in the bibliography published by the Gerontological Society of America, Where do we come from? What are we? Where are we going? Analysis of materials shows that most material cannot be dated or sequenced on the basis of content, that "Spiritual Well-Being" as a concept becomes secularized and individualized, and that meaning and value are seen as personal rather than dialogic with and grounded in collective systems.

163. Tucker, J., & Freeman, S. (1991, Spring). Dance Midrash: Movement exploration inspired by Torah for and about older adults. The Journal of Aging and Judaism, 5, 227-235.

Dance Midrash provides a way to facilitate older adults physically, intellectually, and spiritually as they work together in a Jewish context. Younger participants are guided in the exploration of passages from Torah, in order to gain understanding and sensitivity to matters relating to aging.

Dissertations

164. Feldman, P. S. (1978). Identification of some religious/cultural perceptions of a select population of aging Jewish persons with implications for

Jewish educational programing (Doctor of Philosophy dissertation, University of Pittsburgh). DAI, 40, 911A.

This precisely-titled study has 10 major findings. In brief, the aging Jew looks to his religious cultural group, to its institutions and traditions, to provide ways to meet the exigencies of life and to structure parts of personal and social milieu. As these change, new knowledge may be needed to meet new role demands and to establish new patterns of interaction. Hence there is suggested a specific focus and role for education.

165. Howard, N. I. (1983). Grandfriends: A local church model for personal contact between senior high young people and single elderly persons (Doctor of Ministry thesis, School of Theology at Claremont). DAI, 44, 779A.

This project designed and tested two models to bring young and elderly people into meaningful contact with one another in the life of the local church, to meet the needs of both age groups. A revised model is suggested for adaptation and use in any local church setting.

166. Pipes, B. R. (1981/1982). Christian response to human suffering: A lay theological response to the Book of Job (Doctor of Ministry thesis, Drew University). DAI, 43, 1584A.

Five study sessions on suffering (which focussed on traumatic experiences) revealed that most laity have a theology of suffering but approaches vary widely (punishment for past sins, God sustains, Scripture strengthens, other people strengthen, some withdraw, some seek attention, some live victoriously with debilitating disease, others are crushed by illness). Detailed plans of study and discussion of ministry to suffering people are included.

SOCIAL SERVICES

Books

167. Eastman, P., & Kane, A. (1986). RESPITE: Helping caregivers keep elderly relatives at home, guidelines for a program whose time is now. Washington, DC: National Council of Catholic Women, 42p.

This is a "how to" guide for establishing a church-based RESPITE program of voluntary in-home care for the elderly. It recognizes that "needy families genuinely want to care for their elderly relatives at home, but that, since they are human beings, family members need to be given a chance to refresh their own spirits, to fill their pitchers, so that when they return to the dailiness of their caregiving, they will be renewed spiritually and will be better able to give of themselves with love and understanding" (p.4).

168. Jewish Federation of Metropolitan Chicago. (1966, January). Services to the aged. Chicago: Author.

Although this report is highly specific (i.e. Jewish Federation of Metropolitan Chicago, mid-1960's) the categories of analysis and historical "snap-shot" present clearly the categories of analysis considered important at that time.

169. Leaver, W. (1980). Profile of selected senior citizen programs. Lima, OH: C.S.S., 57p.

This book presents a profile and analysis of programs available for older adults in Florida so that churches and other organizations may be challenged to develop appropriate senior services. The main difference between federally funded social-service programs and church programs was found to be that federally funded programs begin with surveys that identify needed services. Churches usually begin with a group of people who identify their own services. "This is a very important difference in approach. When you begin with services, you get clients or participants. When you begin with people, you get services owned and directed, if not controlled, by the people. The second approach leads to empowerment of people while the first continues service to people" (p.43).

170. Loughhead, E. J. (1987). Eldercare: Starting a center in your church. Nashville, TN: Abingdon, 46p.

This book presents basic information on establishing an adult day-care center in the local church. Contents include: rationale for providing care, preparing the facility, staff recruitment, participant enrollment, scheduling, marketing, and developing a budget.

171. Murphey, J. K. (1986). Sharing care: The Christian ministry of respite care. New York: United Church Press, 58p.

This manual provides all the information necessary for a church or other organization to provide ongoing temporary relief to those who are primary caregivers to the elderly, frail, homebound, or disabled.   It includes a bibliography, resource lists, and sample forms.

172. Shepherd's Centers of America. (1990). Organizational manual for Shepherd's Centers. Kansas City, MO: Author, 124p.

This manual presents steps for establishing a Shepherd's Center, an excellent and successful model for interfaith community organizations dedicated to helping older adults lead productive, creative, meaningful, and interdependent lives. The basic mission of the Shepherd's Centers is older people providing services for older people.

173. Tobin, S. S., Ellor, J. W., & Anderson-Ray, S. M. (1986). Enabling the elderly: Religious institutions within the community service system. Albany, NY: State University of New York Press, 192p.

Opportunities for churches and synagogues to collaborate with social service agencies are presented in this easy to read, practical text. Chapters include: Community Church: An Example of Decision Making in Action; The Well Elderly in the Community; Enabling the Homebound; Outreach to Nursing Home Residents; Living with the Dying; and a Model for Increasing Interaction Among Churches, Synagogues, and Social Agencies.

Articles

174. Anker, L., & Trumbower, J. A. (1985). Congregations reach out to the homebound. Aging, (351), 2-4.

This article describes the Elderly Outreach Program (EOP) which the Catholic Social Services of Albuquerque, New Mexico established in order to encourage local congregations--Catholic and non-Catholic--to develop groups of volunteers to minister to isolated seniors. These volunteers provide friendly visiting, telephone reassurance, help with light chores, transportation, and spiritual ministry. The EOP provides training, technical assistance and consultation to the congregations.

175. Dimmock, A. E. (1983, June 13). Housing the elderly. The

Presbyterian Outlook, 165(24), 9-11.

The author of this article strongly advocates a need for alternative forms of long-term care for the old, especially those over 75 years of age. He urges the churches to design a system linking elderly with needs to elderly with resources in the areas of transportation, meals, personal contact, home repair, home health care, and homemaker service.

176. Ellor, J. W., Thibault, J. M., Netting, F. E., & Carey, C. B. (1990). Wholistic theology as a conceptual foundation for services for the oldest old. Journal of Religious Gerontology, 7(1/2), 99-110.

The authors note that the services provided the old-old reflect our views of human nature. Service to the old-old needs to be based on a wholistic theology that can attend to the human needs of these persons while at the same time affirming their place in the community of faith.

177. Haber, D. (1984, Fall). Church-based mutual help groups for caregivers of non-institutionalized elders. Journal of Religion & Aging, 1(1), 63-69.

A project started with grant funds helped establish mutual help groups at six churches in Washington, DC. A 12-hour training program introduced members to the processes of aging, communication with the elderly, and nursing skills. Reasons for the continuation of three of the six groups are discussed.

178. Haber, D. (1987, Spring/Summer). The Interfaith Volunteer Caregivers Program: A short report. Journal of Religion & Aging, 3(3/4), 151-156.

This article reports on a funded program in Washington, DC for congregation-based caregiving programs and mutual help groups, and a matching program that paired volunteers with isolated older adults.

179. Netting, F. E., Thibault, J. M., & Ellor, J. W. (1988). Spiritual integration: Gerontological interface between the religious and social service communities. Journal of Religion & Aging, 5(1/2), 61-74.

This article examines the interrelationship between the religious and social service sectors that serve aging persons. The linkages between these two sectors are then discussed on three levels: personal, community/local, and institutional/denominational. The first level considers both lower level needs and programs which deal with meaning, the second refers to formal and informal church programs, the third considers changing institutional responses to the changing needs of older persons.

180. Olitzky, K. M. (Ed.). (1988, Fall/Winter). To grow old in Israel: A survey of recent trends and developments [Special issue]. Journal of Aging and Judaism, 3.

Although beyond the geographic limits of this bibliography (USA) the present sociological analysis of Israel's aged and the delivery of services to them is offered as "a beacon of light to all of us scattered throughout world Jewry who strive to treat the elderly within our own midst with deference and honor" (p. 5).

181. Reingold, J., Weiner, A. S., & Holmes, D. (1991, Spring). An analysis of the Jewishness of services to the aged in the United States. The Journal of Aging and Judaism, 5, 177-189.

This article reports on a study of 186 Jewish facilities, programs, and services. Results were analyzed in terms of the strengths and weaknesses of Jewish observance and programming in long-term care facilities and community programs. It is concluded that there has not been adequate recognition of the value of training beyond core topics of Jewish holidays and laws. "If there is a belief that it is the Jewishness of the facilities that creates standards of care and environment then that Jewishness cannot be ignored or minimized" (p. 188).

182. Rosenwaike, I. (1987, Spring/Summer). A demographic profile of the elderly Jewish population in the United States in 1970. The Journal of Aging and Judaism, 1, 126-137.

The patterns and characteristics of the Jewish elderly in 1970 largely paralleled those of the general population. Differences include a relatively high representation of males and thus intact marriages, a relatively higher proportion of persons of advanced educational status, a distinct pattern of geographic distribution of retirees, and a movement to retirement communities.

183. Shapero, S. M. (1987, Spring/summer). Gerontological narcosis. The

Journal of Aging and Judaism, 1, 87-95.

The author argues that the science of gerontology is not being taken seriously by the Jewish community. He notes the obligation and opportunity to develop a viable delivery system for services.

184. Sheehan, N. W. (1989, October). The caregiver information project: A mechanism to assist religious leaders to help family caregivers. The Gerontologist, 29, 703-706.

A 2-1/2 day educational project succeeded in training 200 clergy, lay religious volunteers, and social service providers about issues of caregiving and ways to disseminate information to family caregivers. The program also stimulated the development of caregiver activities and programs.

185. Sheehan, N. W., Wilson, R., & Marella, L. M. (1988, June). The role of the church in providing services for the aging. The Journal of Applied Gerontology, 7, 231-241.

A study indicates that churches and synagogues conceiving their role as one including the social needs of its members tended to offer more church-based aging programs.   Implications suggest that it is important to incorporate gerontological education into seminary training as it may lessen feelings of ageism or gerontophobia which is more difficult to reduce after ordination.

186. Wahlstrom, C. L. (1956).   Religion and the aged. In E. F. Johnson (Ed.), Religion and social work (pp. 113-127). New York: The Institute for Religious and Social Studies.

In the context of social work, the author describes a variety of responses of churches and synagogues to the aged up to 1956: homes for the aged, group programs, services to individuals, and community plans.

Dissertations

187. Huber, L. W. (1985). Connections: A study of the place of the church in the personal networks of the aged (Doctor of Philosphy dissertation, Case Western Reserve University). DAI, 43, 770A.

This dissertation studies the relationship of the church to the personal networks of elderly church members, in order to understand the role of the church in these networks. Offered are tentative guidelines to those in the religious and social service professions about ways of working with the elderly through the churches.

188. Magbee, L. S. (1981). A Presbytery based ministry to the aging of New Orleans (Unpublished Doctor of the Science of Theology dissertation, San Francisco Theological Seminary).

This ministry project studied the aging and social services (church and secular) in the Presbytery of South Louisiana and made recommendations for ministry.

189. Raphael, T. G. (1983). "Rise before the hoary head": Socialization to old age in an Israeli town (Doctor of Philosophy dissertation, Columbia University). DAI, 44, 2512A.

This study of multipurpose senior centers in Safed, Isreal, reveals that four tensions fundamental to Israeli society pervade the clubs and are perpetuated in their programs: a) Judaism vs. Socialist-Zionism, b) social policy formulation vs. application, c) asymmetrical relationship between young and old (in favor of the young), d) men vs. women. The topics of religion, work and images of old age are examined through a study of annual programs. The case method approach to special events in organization life may be applicable to the study of other social service agencies (including churches and synagogues in the USA).

INSTITUTIONAL CARE OF THE AGED

Books

190. Abbot, J. W. (Ed.). (1988). Hospice resource manual for local churches. New York: Pilgrim Press, 90p.

This manual clearly explains the hospice movement, why Christians should be involved in the movement, levels of church involvement, model programs, funding problems and resources, and care reimbursement. While hospice care is not age specific, older adults and those who plan ministry programs for older adults in local churches need to know about it.

191. Beck, C. L., & Burow, E. (Eds.). (1988). <u>Bless Bible studies: Bringing life experience to scripture study</u>. Minneapolis, MN: Augsburg.

This unique four part Bible study series is designed to be used with nursing home and health care residents of various religious backgrounds and traditions. Each set contains a leader manual and large print participant leaflet. <u>Blessed by Jesus</u> examines basic human needs: trust, faith, friendship, anger, being cared for, preparing for death. <u>Blessed by the God of Abraham, Isaac and Jacob</u> connects Old Testament personalities to New Testament promises. <u>Blessed by the Spirit</u> explores human emotions and God's actions through themes of loneliness, suffering, comforting, value and worth. <u>Seasonal studies</u> has sessions based on the liturgical calendar.

192. Cassidy, H., & Flaherty, L. (1982). <u>Caring relationships: Guide for families of nursing home residents</u>. Minneapolis, MN: Augsburg, 24p.

This small booklet is written for family members who have recently placed a relative in a nursing home. It deals briefly with factors that influence the adjustment of the resident to the nursing home, and offers suggestions for developing conversation, expanding the memory, supporting the withdrawn, dealing with grief, coping with misdirected anger, listening and responding.

193. Hynes, M. R. (1989). <u>Ministry to the aging</u>. Collegeville, MN: Liturgical, 56p.

This booklet covers topics such as understanding the aging process, ageism, teaching the elderly, praying with the elderly, and ministering to the physical needs of the elderly. It is written for those who care for elderly in their home or nursing home.

194. Irion, P. E. (1988). <u>Hospice and ministry</u>. Nashville, TN: Abingdon, 224p.

Written from a Christian perspective, this book treats the relation of hospice to Christian ministry. Although not specifically for older persons, this book is included as a guide for pastoral care given in a hospice setting rather than techniques for dealing with the terminally ill and their families. The book considers spiritual/religious issues of hospice patients and families, openness in dealing with death, pain control and the pastor, the blend of professional and lay caregivers, and the attitudes and roles of the pastor.

195. Keys, J. T.   (1983).   Our older friends: A guide for visitors. Philadelphia, PA: Fortress, 64p.

This book is intended to serve as a guide for people who are preparing to spend time with older, often invalid persons.

196. Murphy, P. (1979). Healing with time and love: A guide for visiting the elderly. Los Angeles, CA: University of Southern California, 47p.

This little booklet about convalescent homes will aid friendly visitors, nursing home personnel, and friends and families of long term care residents.   It describes the convalescent home setting, presents a profile of the elderly resident, and outlines suggestions for visiting the frail elderly.

Articles

197. Byrne, S. M.   (1985).   A zest for life!   Journal of Gerontological Nursing, 11, 30-33.

Gerontological nurse specialists need to recognize the importance of the religious dimension in the patient's life and how this aspect contributes to life satisfaction.   Assessment interviews provide information about the effect a patient's religious beliefs have on his or her need for achievement and purpose in life, feelings of self-worth, and for love and belonging.

198. Clayton, J. (1991, Summer). Let there be life: An approach to worship with Alzheimer's patients and their families. The Journal of Pastoral Care, 65, 177-179.

This article describes a worship service based on activities using the feeling functions of the right-brain. The service uses a format which S. V. Doughty suggests in his book Ministry of love (see citation 46):   brief scripture passages, familiar hymns, and prayer. No message, sermon, or talk is used since the logical functions of the left-brain are needed to interpret the "message"--a function memory impaired elders may no longer easily access.

199. Cohen-Mansfield, J., & Rabinovich, B. A. (1990, Winter). Religious beliefs and practices of elderly Jewish nursing home residents. The Journal of Aging and Judaism, 5, 87-94.

A study of religious beliefs and practices of elderly Jewish nursing home residents supports general findings in the literature about the religiousity of women, the effect of the time periods, and beliefs of immigrants. Implications are drawn for the design of programs in nursing homes.

200. Devine, B. A. (1980, November). Attitudes of the elderly toward religion. Journal of Gerontological Nursing, 6, 679-687.

An analysis of elderly attitudes determines the attitudinal change toward religion after retirement (little change); the effect of religious denomination, sex, age, health, past experience, marital status, and geographic location on religious activity; and the value of religion and religious communities as support groups. The author found that religion and religious communities offer comfort and are a source of meaning for older persons. The article recommends that nurses should consider the importance of religion for the elderly.

201. Dilworth-Anderson, P. (1981, September/October). A social structure that works: The case of Green Nursing Home. Aging, 39-41.

A study of the Green Nursing Home in Evanston, Illinois, describes a nursing home where residents live in a home-like atmosphere, maintaining some control over their lives and experiencing a high level of morale. Residents were allowed and encouraged to pursue activities off the premises, and they were not discriminated against for forming a complaint group.

202. Ellor, J. W., Stettner, J., & Spath, H. (1987). Ministry with the confused elderly. Journal of Religion & Aging, 4(2), 21-33.

A study of appropriate ministry with older adults who have Organic Brain Syndromes presents a model that combines sensory stimulation, reality orientation, and worship to provide a focal point for ministry with the confused elderly. This model is particularly useful in long-term care institutions, and may be used successfully by anyone comfortable with leading worship. An appendix lists a suggested order of worship, possible hymns, and appropriate Bible verses.

203. Friedman, D. A. (1987, Spring/Summer). The Mitzvah model: A therapeutic resource for the institutionalized aged. The Journal of Aging and

Judaism, 1, 96-108.

The author appeals to the concept of Mitzvah or religious obligation which allows for adaptation as having the potential for ameliorating the sense of worthlessness of older persons living in institutions. Mitzvah is accessible even to the impaired, frail person. The individual Jewish person is bound to the convenant and commandments, and the redemption of the Jewish people as a whole depends on the collective fulfillment of the covenant. Self-esteem and social regard are intimately connected to the concept of religious obligation. The author discusses ways of using Mitzvah therapeutically in the nursing home.

204. Ginsburg, I. (1980, May/June). Religion for the aged. Nursing Homes, 29, 28-30, 32-33.

The author discusses the personal character of religious emotions. These feelings tend to foster a sense of security and fulfillment. Religious activity may have a therapeutic value. The religious involvement of older people, particularly in long-term care facilities, is important as it improves the quality of a resident's existence. Educational, social, and religious activities must provide support for maintaining healthy minds.

205. Guttman, D. (1990, Summer). Caring for frail Jewish aged--Myth and reality. The Journal of Aging and Judaism, 4, 271-288.

This article deals with the refutation of shared social myths that 1) the rate of institutionalization of frail elderly Jews is much higher than it has been before, 2) that there will be a shortage of caretakers for the frail elderly, 3) that mobility is an impediment to caregiving, and 4) that, unlike in the past, the frail elderly are now seldom cared for by their siblings.

206. Haitsma, K. V. (1986). Intrinsic religious orientation: Implications in the study of religiosity and personal adjustment in the aged. The Journal of Social Psychology, 126(5), 685-687.

This particular research study of retirement home residents over age 60 (who proved to be a highly intrinsic population satisfied with their lives) suggests that religious orientation may be a significant concept for studying personal adjustment of the elderly.

207. Hawkins, D. G. (1987). Understanding and managing Alzheimer's disease. Journal of Religion & Aging, 4(2), 35-45.

A clear description of Alzheimer's disease and its effects on victim and caregiver leads to a series of pastoral strategies for working with caregivers and pastoral care workers.

208. Hubbard, R. W. (1979, December). Pastoral care in the nursing home: Guidelines for communication with institutionalized elderly. The Journal of Pastoral Care, 33, 239-242.

Eight fairly straightforward communication guidelines are illustrated in two case examples, one of which is a therapeutic religious service for nursing home residents.

209. Huth, M. J. (1983, December/1984, January). A seminary becomes a residence and community for the elderly. Aging, (342), 22-25.

St. Leonard's Center in Centerville, Ohio is an example of a collaboration between religious and community organizations to create a congregate living facility for the elderly. This Center developed after St. Leonard's Seminary for Franciscan Priests closed. In addition to residential apartments for the elderly, day programs for people of different ages, creeds, races and physical and mental abilities were established and a section of the seminary converted to bedrooms for people on spiritual or professional retreats.

210. Koening, H. G., Bearon, L. B., & Dayringer, R. (1989). Physician perspectives on the role of religion in the physician-older patient relationship. The Journal of Family Practice, 28, 441-448.

A research study of 160 middle aged, racially and regionally homogenous, male family physicians and general practictioners found that the majority of these physicians acknowledged the influence of religion in the lives of older adults--that religion affects mental health and perhaps physical health positively. Younger physicians were more receptive than older physicians to addressing religious issues with patients. The physician's beliefs and attitudes appeared to be important in determining their willingness to discuss religious issues with patients and consequently, whether patients brought up such issues during the medical visit.

211. Leviatan, U. (1989, Winter). Successful aging: The Kibbutz experience. The Journal of Aging and Judaism, 4, 71-92.

Although the focus of this article is outside the geographical limits of this bibliography, the emphasis on learning from successful experiences rather than from correction of failures is applicable in our context.

212. Minnery, T. (1981). Christian retirement homes: A rest along the way. Christianity Today, 25, 583-86.

This article challenges conservative Christians to establish nursing homes and retirement communities where residents are treated as individuals and human dignity is maximized. These homes can help dissipate the greatest fear of the older residents--the fear of dying.

213. Moore, R. J., & Newton, J. H. (1977). Attitudes of the life threatened hospitalized elderly. Essence, 1, 129-138.

One finding of this quantitative research study of terminally ill elderly patients, their primary caregivers and family members revealed that denial functioned as patients' main method of coping with the reality of death. This finding was based on the fact that many of the patients failed to admit the importance of religion in determining their attitudes toward death. Patients, family members, and staff all preferred that a doctor inform them of the severity of their illness.

214. Nelson, F. L. (1977, Summer). Religiosity and self-destructive crises in the institutionalized elderly. Suicide and Life Threatening Behavior, 7, 67-74.

This exploration of the relationship between religiosity and self-destructive behavior focuses on the intensity of religious commitment rather than religious affiliation. The author finds that intensity of religious commitment is a more meaningful indication of religiosity than is church attendance. Indirect life threatening behavior and intensity of religious commitment tend to vary inversely.

215. Netting, F. E. (1987). Religiously affiliated continuum of care retirement communities. Journal of Religion & Aging, 4(1), 51-66.

This study illustrates a wide variety of structural relationships in religious continuum of care retirement communities. Types include: the religious order model, the single congregational model, the multiple congregational model, the interfaith model, the religious community leaders model, the denominational model, and the corporate intermediary model.

216. Netting, F. E., & Wilson, C. C. (1987). Educating professionals to understand religious sponsorship of long term care facilities. Gerontology & Geriatrics Education, 7, 25-35.

A teaching model for presenting the implications of church or synagogue sponsorship of retirement communities and/or nursing homes to religious and health care professionals, this three-hour session consists of 1) theoretical perspectives of voluntary sponsorship, 2) issues involved in long term care facilities and religious sponsorship, and 3) strategies for change.

217. Netting, F. E., & Wilson, C. C. (1987, Spring/Summer). When religion and health care meet: The church-related home. Journal of Religion & Aging, 3(3/4), 101-114.

This article describes current numbers and locations of church homes in the United States and proposes a model for analysis of church-related organizations. Issues include sound management, high technology, projected life spans of residents, and secularization. In a related article in the same issue, Netting does a case study of the secularization of a church-related social service agency for the elderly.

218. Paterson, G. W. (1984, Fall). The pastoral care of persons in pain. Journal of Religion & Aging, 1(1), 17-30.

This article, while not specifically addressing pain in elderly persons, may provide clergy, chaplains, and pastoral counselors with a better understanding of the three types of pain: acute, chronic, and terminal. The author presents several Judeo-Christian views on the meaning of pain and suffering.

219. Peterson, E. A. (1985). The physical...the spiritual...can you meet all of your patient's needs? Journal of Gerontological Nursing, 11(10), 23-27.

This article discusses the importance of assessing the spiritual needs of gerontological patients. Spiritual needs encompass whatever provides a sense of meaning and purpose to a person's life, a source of forgiveness, and a source of love and relatedness. Providing spiritual care involves being present and willing to share in the changes and struggles in the lives of patients.

220. Richards, M., & Seicol, R. S. (1991). The challenge of maintaining spiritual connectedness for persons institutionalized with dementia. Journal of Religious Gerontology, 7(3), 27-40.

This article stresses the need to recognize and minister to spiritual needs in persons institutionalized because of dementia. The authors discuss memory, spirituality and grief, care planning, communication, and education of caregivers.

221. Schulze, E. J., & Engle, V. F. (1987, Spring/Summer). A partnership of care: Support systems for families of institutionalized older adults. Journal of Religion & Aging, 3(3/4), 91-99.

A description of five programs at a nursing home sponsored by a Moravian church. The programs reflect a partnership of care among residents, families, and staff. Programs are initial and discharge care planning, orientation to the nursing home, a spouse support group, a companionship for the dying program and a family support group.

222. Schwanke, E. R. (1986, Spring). Providing pastoral care for the elderly in long term care facilities without a chaplain utilizing coordinated congregational resources. Journal of Religion & Aging, 2(3), 57-64.

This article reports how 12 Lutheran congregations worked out a plan to provide the necessary pastoral care for nearly 700 residents in six long term care facilities.

223. Shour, A. (1990, Spring). The aging Holocaust survivor in the institution. The Journal of Aging and Judaism, 4, 141-160.

This study compared the reactions of Holocaust survivors living in an institution (Jewish Home for the Aged) to reactions of residents who had not experienced the trauma of the Holocaust first-hand. The reactions of the two groups were found to be comparable, thus stressing the importance of sensitivity to and understanding of individual needs of residents.

224. Simmons, H. C. (1991, Summer). "Teach us to pray": Pastoral care of the new nursing home resident. Journal of Pastoral Care, 45, 169-175.

This article explores prayer and devotion at a specific and traumatic point in the life of many older adults, namely entrance into a long-term care facility, and inquires about appropriate pastoral care at that moment. The moment is particularly traumatic because it involves leaving behind the home in which the person is his or her normal self, working through feelings of anger, uselessness, and loneliness, and coming to reorder life in a new setting unlike any other ever known. Appropriate pastoral care at this point in life is summed up in the phrase, "Teach us to pray".

225. Stevens, W. F. (1991). Christian life emphasis in the retirement community: A Koinonia of spiritual awareness. Journal of Religious Gerontology, 7(4), 55-85.

This article describes a retirement community which seeks to fulfill a deliberate requirement that faith in Christ is an integral part of resident life. Christian Life Emphasis involves a variety of bonding rituals and a ministry of resident to resident that enables spiritual awareness to permeate life throughout the continuum of care. An appendix presents brief Christian Life Emphasis Services of commitment, blessing of a room, acceptance of a new resident, nursing care communion, and "a service of upholding for a resident moving from independent living to nursing care" (p. 88).

226. Surrey, P. J. (1981, July). Until she dies. . . Christian Ministry, 12, 31-33.

In this essay, an Episcopal pastor suggests that ministers visiting parishioners in nursing homes can come with a positive view rather than the negative doom and gloom view that nursing home residents are simply waiting to die. His positive list of suggestions for the role of the pastor includes visiting weekly, administering communion when asked, and enrolling lay people of all ages for visitation.

Dissertations

227. Greene, R. R. (1980/1981). Ageism and death anxiety as related to geriatric social work as a career choice (Doctor of Philosophy dissertation, University of Maryland). DAI, 42, 858A.

This study explored some factors related to the career choice of social work with the aged. In general the variables found to be most closely associated with career choice in geriatric social work were the social worker's positive attachment to an older person when growing up and fear of dying of others. Religious affiliation and religiosity were not significant variables between the group that chose to work with the aging and those who did not.

228. Halstead, H. L. (1982). Self-perceived well being among retired older adults: The positive side of aging (Doctor of Philosophy dissertation, Kansas State University). DAI, 43, 2855B.

This study of 72 persons (a random sample) in an urban retirement center revealed a high level of contentment among residents, a positive sense of spiritual well-being, a positive attitude about physical health status in spite of physical disease, and a prevailing sense of feeling younger than chronological age.

229. Pardue, L. (1989). Models for ministry: The spiritual needs of frail elderly living in long-term-care facilities. Mars Hill College, Ashville, NC.

This research study compares the perception of pastoral needs between residents of three long-term-care facilities and their pastors. The residents said unanimously that what helped them move through impact and recoil to reorganization and adaptation was personal prayer. The pastors, on the other hand, thought that the need was for communal worship, for collective activities. Clergy "view collective activities as the foundations for all functions. For the residents, collective activities seem to be de-emphasized until the final stage of reorganization" (p. 32).

230. Smith, T. K. (1979). Pastoral ministry and the needs of the aging (Doctor of Ministry thesis, School of Theology at Claremont). DAI, 40, 1536A.

Within a broad context of the church's response to the aging in society, this project studies the pastoral role as exercised in a nursing home in Hawaii, using case studies.

231. Walker, A. R. (1981). <u>A course of study for the elderly in a retirement high-rise community</u> (Doctor of Ministry thesis, Drew University). <u>DAI</u>, <u>42</u>, 4384A.

This project developed a course of study for church members who live in a local high-rise retirement complex which would--using Henri Nouwen's "Redemptive Theory" approach to education--enhance the participants' sense of worth. The enlisting of participants is identified as the most difficult phase of the project because of the reluctance of elderly adults to participate in any demanding approach to education.

Empowerment

Books

232. Anderson, J. D. (1986). <u>Taking heart: Empowering older adults for community ministries, a handbook</u>. Washington, DC: Cathedral College of the Laity, 88p.

This resource handbook is written "to help older persons give direction and meaning to their lives so that personal significance and meaning is increased and so they can enhance the good contribution they are making to the world about them" (p. v). The first section discusses the nature of empowerment, the second gives workshop designs for life review and for vision formation. The workshop designs are both specific and adaptable.

233. Ellison, J. (1973). <u>The last third of life club</u>. Philadelphia, PA: Pilgrim, 157p.

This book stands well outside the mainstream of inspirational and common-sensical devotional literature of the 1970s. The group faces death squarely, sees that the "eventual passage from this life" can be a glory rather than a dread, and resolves to use the years that remain to prepare for death. Through daily meditation, life review, choice of new life goals, and a growing cosmic awareness the Last Third of Life Club members are able to embrace life.

234. Fahey, C., & Wakin, E. (1984). <u>A Catholic guide to the mature years</u>. Huntington, IN: Our Sunday Visitor.

This book stresses, in an inspirational and common-sensical way, some of the opportunities of the "third age" (i.e. the last third of life) when people "plan, adjust, and discover how they can get the most out of it in the spirit of Christian fulfillment" (p. 6). Included are chapters on the greying of the parish, working for justice, and growing in holiness.

235. Gray, R. H. (1985). Survival of the spirit: My detour through a retirement home. Atlanta, GA: John Knox, 94p.

Excerpts from a diary written in her 85th year reveal a woman's struggle to maintain her individuality and personhood in a retirement home in the face of inflexible and insensitive administrators. The author and her peers emerge as positive, creative, but embattled people.

236. Hessel, D. T. (Ed.). (1979). Age in a new age: Study/action guide for Maggie Kuhn on aging. New York: Program Agency, UPCUSA, 48p.

A carefully designed and tested study guide to be used in a variety of ways by groups engaging in strategies of analysis and change.

237. Hessel, D. (Ed.). (1981). Empowering ministry in an ageist society. Atlanta, GA: Presbyterian Office on Aging, 92p.

This volume presents edited talks given at the Princeton Symposium on Aging by Maggie Kuhn, Carroll Estes, Heije Faber, Richard Shaull, and Dieter Hessel. Four areas of concern and action addressed at the symposium were: seminary education, community services, pension and retirement, and shared housing. Recommendations made at the symposium are summarized in the appendix.

238. Hoffman, M. A. (1985). The older we get...an action guide to social change. Boston, MA: Unitarian Universalist Service Committee, 138p.

This manual is for groups interested in advocacy about issues of aging. It looks at facts and fictions about aging, one's own aging, and initiating change at both the local and national levels. It includes an appendix listing national organizations, audio-visual resources, and a reading list.

239. Jones, M. (1988). <u>Growing old: The ultimate freedom</u>. New York: Human Sciences, 116p.

This book is a substantial contribution to the literature of aging, freedom, support groups, and spirituality by a social ecologist and psychiatrist. Social learning (including personal growth, old age, and mysticism) requires periodic exposure to a supportive and highly motivated peer group. With this support, "retirement" may become "freedom" to change, to set priorities based on contemplation, to question social stereotypes, to engage in social critique, and so on. The author also addresses death, spirituality, contemplation, and the quest for truth.

240. Kleyman, P. (1974). <u>Senior power: Growing old rebelliously</u>. San Francisco, CA: Glide, 177p.

This is a personal, anecdotal, and practical history of a group of seniors at San Francisco's Glide Memorial Methodist Church. Their early organizing activities helped form the California Legislative Council of Older Americans.

241. Maitland, D. J. (1991). <u>Aging as counterculture: A vocation for the later years</u>. New York: Pilgrim, 185p.

This book seeks to answer the question: "What are the distinctive possibilities in aging" (p.13)? The title of the book indicates clearly its thrust and dynamic. Chapter titles are: Spirituality in aging: Regaining one's balance; Experience and faith; Life's "morning:" The forward thrust; Unclaimed lives; Aging as counterculture; Aging as God's design. This book could form the basis for an older adult study group.

242. Manser, N. (1984). <u>Older people have choices: Information for decisions about health, home and money</u>. Minneapolis, MN: Augsburg, 32p.

Written under the auspices of the Division for Life and Mission in the Congregation and the Board of Publication of the American Lutheran Church, this resource is designed to help older persons remain independent as long as possible through changes that occur in late life by presenting options as well as how to assess them. Topics discussed are family and friends, finances, changes in residence, dementia, and guardianship. While designed for individuals, this resource could provide a starting point for group study.

243. Maves, P. B. (1951). The best is yet to be. Philadelphia, PA: Westminster, 96p.

Although the Forward states that this is not "another self-help, you-can-do-it-if-you-will, lift-yourself-up-by-your-bootstraps, and let-God-do-it-type of book," it seems to this annotater that all these characteristics are present in some degree. Written in 1951, this book speaks frankly about old age and its challenges, offers hope and promise, and speaks a word of Gospel meditation. What sets this book aside from other less successful books of this genre is perhaps the author's wide range of knowledge and his dedication to aging which would be shown over another 40 years.

244. Maves, P. B. (Ed.). (1984). A ministry to match the age: Empowering older adults in United Methodist Churches. Cincinnati, OH: General Board of Global Ministries, United Methodist Church, 78p.

The National Consultation of Older Adults in The United Methodist Church, of which this is the report, "sought to find ways to deepen and expand the awareness of the total membership of The United Methodist Church to the needs and potential of its older members, to identify issues and concerns of major importance to them, to determine the role and responsibility they wished to assume in representing these issues and concerns in the life of The United Methodist Church, and to develop specific recommendations and strategies for implementation" (p. 1).

245. National Council of Jewish Women. (1983). Self help for seniors. New York: Author, 30p.

This guide suggests how to create self-help mutual aid groups among older adults. Essentially, it explains how to form groups, recruit participants, and train facilitators.

Articles

246. Dickerson, B. E., & Myers, D. R. (1988). The contributory and changing roles of older adults in the Church and Synagogue. Educational Gerontology, 14, 303-314.

The authors describe three extramural roles (advocate, mediator, and missionary) and three intramural roles (intergenerational specialist, religious educator, and encourager) as examples of ways in which the "new older person is uniquely empowered to contribute to the mission of religious organizations and, in return, receive an enhanced sense of spiritual well-being" (p. 305). Barriers to the contribution of older adults include age grading, structural requirements (e.g. regularity of attendance) for admission to contributory roles, and the definition of "family" as "married couple" rather than shared faith or joint affiliation.

247. Hiatt, L. G. (1986, Fall). Low technology for maximizing independence. Generations, 11(1).

Essays in this issue of Generations look at new and future technological developments for maintaining or increasing the independence of older persons. Some of these technological trends are designed to increase mobility, expand agility, enhance vision and hearing, and improve memory and mental functioning. Articles look at the problems of bringing gerontologists and technologists together, the effect of technology on older people, utilizing aerospace technology, choosing the right device, and decreasing risks to the older driver.

248. Kastenbaum, R. (1990). The age of saints and the saintliness of age. International Journal of Aging and Human Development, 30, 95-118.

This article examines historical data on the age of male and female saints. Four hypotheses are examined about the possible age-saint relationship. The last section of the article inquires about the appropriateness of saintliness as a model for old age, specifically the person converted to sainthood. "A life-time of experience and the changed circumstances associated with aging could open the way to an altered perspective on self, world, and God" (p. 115) inspired by the example of the saints. This contrasts with current age-based health rationing concepts.

249. Maves, P. B. (n. d.). They shall bring forth fruit in age. 15p.

Written about 1950, this article-length pamphlet (in a series called "Parishioners Are People") describes the problems and potentialities of an older society. Written by Paul Maves near the beginning of his long and distinguished career in aging, this brief pamphlet allows a glimpse of his early perceptions of old age in his social context.

250. Simmons, H. C.   (1989, November).   Ministry with older adults: Freedom in old age. Professional Approaches for Christian Educators, 49-53.

This second article in a series on ministry with older adults identifies freedom as a fundamental issue of human life and religious educational ministry in the United States. Freedom issues assume a characteristic, unique shape in old age. Specifically, as the culture begins to marginalize older adults because they no longer meet the cultural norms for authentic humanity, older adults are increasingly free to form a counter-collective judgment about the nature and worth of old age. Thus they may begin to embody a vision of the human that does not require an unequal distribution of power and goods.   Specific educational strategies are suggested, namely peer reflection and shared action.

251. Simmons, H. C. (1988). Religious education of older adults: A present and future perspective. Educational Gerontology, 14, 279-289.

This article examines current religious education for older adults and finds it lacking in its failure to promote collective meaning. The analysis of the present distinctiveness of old age is loss of meaning; this is understood through concepts of class domination.   The author proposes face-to-face groupings of older adults who in recognizing their common oppression come to claim their own agency and to commit to social change.

252. Tittle, C. R. (1983). Religiosity and deviance: Toward a contingency theory of constraining effects. Social Forces, 61, 653-682.

Although this article does not focus on age in any substantial way, it may provide a theoretical framework for understanding the role of religion in producing or not producing countercultural behaviors in old age. Specifically the article concludes that "individual religiousity seems to inhibit deviance most within secularized, disorganized social contexts because those environments do not possess the mechanisms necessary to produce general conformity, thereby permitting focused effects for the variables linked with religious participation" (p. 676).

Dissertations

253. Nisbet, D. E. (1984). Social activism among the aging: An empirical study of its attitudinal-ideological and personality correlates (Doctor of Philosophy dissertation, State University of New York at Buffalo). DAI, 45,

2620A.

This study of 478 Gray Panthers is the first empirical inquiry into social advocacy by and on behalf of the elderly.   The results indicate that the movement's major support comes from two groups with different motivations. Older Gray Panthers appear mobilized by a sense of decremental deprivation, while younger Gray Panthers appear drawn to the cause by a desire that the elderly share in the benefits of American life.   The younger are also drawn to social advocacy for the old by a general need to be actively involved in social causes; the elderly Gray Panther activist is often motivated to be active only in his or her own cause.

Ethics

GENERAL AND SPECIFIC ETHICAL QUESTIONS

Books

254. American values as expressed in national policy on aging. (1981). National Symposium on Spiritual & Ethical Value System Concerns [October, 27, 1980]. Athens, GA: The National Interfaith Coalition on Aging, 56p.

This remarkable historical document records some important discussion about spiritual and ethical values in 1980. These are the minutes of a hearing before the National Symposium on Spiritual and Ethical Value System Concerns in the 1981 WHCoA, convened by the National Interfaith Coalition on Aging. Witnesses include Rabbi Siegel, Dr. Andrew Achenbaum, Rev. Jerry Smart, Mrs. Dell Hagan, Dr. Harry R. Moody, Ms. Ann Egan, Mrs. Mary Martin, Rev. Earl Kragnes and others. A companion volume of background reading includes a symposium working bibliography.

255. Applebaum, R. (1989, Winter). Assuring quality of care. Generations, 13(1).

Essays from a variety of perspectives and disciplines address three major topics on the subject of quality of care in home, nursing home, hospital, and foster care: 1) defining quality, 2) the balance of cost and quality concerns, and 3) the development of a research base to undergird the design of quality assurance strategies.

256. Bayer, R., Caplan, A., Dubler, N. N., & Zuckerman, C.   (1987, Summer).   Coercive placement of elders: Protection or choice?   Generations, 11(4).

Essays in this issue address the following problems: ethical dilemmas in nursing home placement, the appropriateness of using the Mental Status Examination for assessing the capacity to function of elderly persons, extending due process protection for the mentally ill to elderly patients approaching nursing home placement, and the response of nursing home ombudsmen to the challenge of undesired institutionalization.   Two case studies are presented and followed with views from a medical anthropologist, an attorney, a social worker, and a philosopher.   Guidelines for practitioners and recommendations for balancing the social welfare and advocacy perspectives conclude the issue.

257. Cole, T. R., & Ellor, J. W. (Eds.).   (1990, Fall).   Aging and the human spirit.   Generations, 14(4).

In 20 brief articles this issue of Generations approaches its subject from a wide variety of perspectives: the meaning of age, long-term care and the human spirit, the transitoriness of human existence, the Islamic vision of aging and death, art and artists, theology, liturgy and ceremony, programs, personal narrative, and the integration of spiritual concerns into social services.   The articles, although brief, often accomplish real depth.

258. Cole, T. R., & Gadow, S. A. (Eds.).   (1986).   What does it mean to grow old?   Durham, NC: Duke University Press, 301p.

Prominent scholars from various disciplines of the humanities (philosophy, history, theology, sociology, law) reflect on the meaning of aging and death. The perspectives from which they begin allow them to grasp some profoundly human aspects of aging which have an openness to the dimension of life often referred to as "religious."

259. Hayes, C. L. (Ed.).   (Spring 1985).   Ethics and aging [Special issue]. Social Thought, 11(2).

This issue presents four papers given at an Ethics and Aging Conference in November 1984.   Included are responses to the papers.   Bartholomew J. Collopy, "Medicare: Ethical Issues in Public Policy for the Elderly;" Edward J. Ryle, "The Aging, Income Support Programs, and Economic Well-Being:

A Catholic Perspective;" Charles E. Curran, "Filial Responsibility for an Elderly Parent;" Laurence B. McCullough, "Long-Term Care for the Elderly: An Ethical Analysis".

260. Lawton, M. P., & Weeden, J. (1985, Spring). Housing. Generations, 9(3).

These articles present issues related to housing all socio-economic groups: the history of public housing, housing policy, home equity conversion, retirement communities, continuum of care retirement communities for mid-upper income elders, who pays for congregate housing, expansion and improvement in board and care housing, vanishing hotels for low-income elders, accessory apartments, respite care, shelters for homeless elders, the cost effectiveness of homesharing programs, and the meaning of "home" for elders.

261. Moody, H. R. (Ed.). (1985, Winter). Ethics and aging. Generations, 10(2).

This issue includes essays on: the role of ethics in clarifying discussion; the lack of any meaning given to aging by our culture; the place of wisdom in the controversy over the definition of competency; the decision to stop giving food and water to terminally ill elders; elder abuse and neglect; a taxonomy of issues in long term care; resolving dilemmas of conflicting professional opinions; research in geriatrics; the withholding of scarce medical resources from the old on the basis of age.

Articles

262. Bockle, F. (1975). Theological-ethical aspects of aging. Theology Digest, 23, 235-240.

Bockle compares the earlier optimism of a theology of aging with more realistic contemporary views of sickness, aging, and death. He argues that old age cannot simply be viewed using a deficit model: growing old and dying are normal phases of human life.

263. Callahan, S. (1978, June). Regulating an anti-aging drug: commentary. The Hastings Center Report, 8, 19-20.

Reflecting on the early testing of an anti-age drug (Sinemort), the author asks the ethical questions about who should decide risks and benefits, who should control the anti-aging pill, and should we legitimate anti-aging medication. She recommends the formation of an appointed interdisciplinary group, and indicates the testimony she would offer such a group: it is good to live and bad to die, and science is liberating and essential. A second author raises several objections and is, on the whole, less positive.

264. Chambers, C. D., Pribble, K. S., & Harter, M. T. (1986, Fall/Winter). Biomedical ethics in the year 2000: O = f(H.E.F.). Journal of Religion & Aging, 3(1/2), 47-61.

The authors propose that the reality of old (O) is a function (f) of one's health status (H), one's economic status (E), and one's level of fear (F). As more elderly live longer and use increasingly more public resources, access to these resources will be restricted and the elderly will be placed at ever increasing levels of risk. The authors also present the history, current status, and future projections for elderly health and health care.

265. Dresner, S. H. (1987, Winter). Geriatric sex and the Jews. The Journal of Aging and Judaism, 2, 94-107.

This article is based on an exchange of letters between an executive of the Council for the Jewish Elderly and Rabbi Samuel Dresner. Rabbi Dresner takes a strong stand in maintaining the sancity of marriage, even in a nursing home. He raises the question whether the Jewish community has the right and responsibility to preserve Jewish sexual ethics within institutions sponsored and funded by the Jewish community.

266. Enelow, H. (1991, Spring). The religion of old age. The Journal of Aging and Judaism, 5, 241-246.

This sermon, printed in 1935, stresses respect for old age. In particular, respect is merited by righteousness, the need to retire at an appropriate age in order to work for the common good and such public service as leisure alone makes possible, the need for optimism based on religion, and a religious calmness about approaching death.

267. Gordon, M. A. (1984, January/February). Rabbinic comment: Old age:

Right to privacy and patient's right to know. The Mount Sinai Journal of Medicine, 51, 89-91.

Traditional Judaism does not mandate securing informed consent although this is a moral issue. Informed consent is a means for physicians and patients to communicate about treatment so that the patient can choose a course of therapy and the physician advocate a desired course of therapy. On the right to know, the author argues that the key issues are the wisdom, necessity, and purpose of imparting information. The balance should be between upsetting a patient needlessly and leaving the patient without time to prepare for death.

268. Gribetz, D. (1984, January/February). End of life: Discussion. The Mount Sinai Journal of Medicine, 51, 92-100.

Several physicians and rabbis discuss medical and Jewish religious positions regarding autopsy, the donation of organs, and needle biopsies. Briefly discussed also are the mandatory donation of organs, and embalming; care of the elderly; treatment decisions (in medical cases involving children, the elderly and the incompetent); and the physician's role as giver of courage, strength and fortitude.

269. Heinecken, M. J. (1985, Fall/1985-86, Winter). Exchanging metaphors between science and religion: Constructs which shape the church's response. Journal of Religion & Aging, 2(1/2), 17-27.

This article proposes a contextual ethic framed by six basic affirmations articulated within a Lutheran tradition: 1) the unconditional love of God to all creatures, 2) the sinfulness of all human beings, 3) the justification of sinners by faith alone without the works of the law, 4) the necessary distinction and interrelation between justice and love, 5) the civil righteousness of which all human beings are capable, and 6) the individual's stance towards life. Ethical decisions are to be made in the light of these principles and in light of contemporary secular scientific knowledge.

270. Klinefelter, D. S. (1984). Aging, autonomy, and the value of life. Journal of Applied Gerontology, 1(3), 7-19.

This study in bioethics addresses a cluster of moral, social, religious, political, and economic issues which are part of the world of the old in the late 20th century. Specifically, the author studies ethical and religious dimensions of the relationship between freedom and dependence, sickness and health, and meaning and value. He suggests an ideal of "dependence with dignity" in the face of prevailing images of aging as illness, disease, and decline.

271. Linzer, N., & Lowenstein, L. (1987, Fall). Autonomy and paternalism in work with the frail Jewish elderly. The Journal of Aging and Judaism, 2, 19-34.

The authors first present a theoretic framework for analyzing the tension between autonomy and paternalism; then they describe a small independent project (Project Ezra) in which this tension is played out. The elderly are frail and limited. They would, perhaps, give over their autonomy to the staff. But the staff is guided 1) by the principles of Tzedakah which stress the relationship between the individual and responsibilities in the community and 2) by principles of social work which value self-determination. Resolution of the tension between autonomy and paternalism is found in the idea that neither autonomy nor community are absolutes.

272. Lyon, K. B. (1988). Aging in theological perspective. Educational Gerontology, 14, 243-254.

This article investigates three themes of Jewish and Christian theological traditions: 1) the blessing of age (i.e., that loss is not all that there is to age, and that there should be a focus on values associated with age rather than on the sins of youth); 2) aging, oppression, and the justice of God (i.e., that values must be promoted which reflect God's love and demand for justice for all persons); and 3) the religio-moral responsibilities of older adults (i.e., that old age is not an extended moral holiday). These themes are investigated in their historic formulations and as they enter into conversation with present realities of aging.

273. Moberg, D. O. (1979). Ethical dimensions of aging. In P. C. Cotham (Ed.), Christian social ethics (pp. 169-185). Grand Rapids, MI: Baker Book House.

After describing the lives and social situations of older adults, the author calls attention to a few ethical principles derived from scripture that might guide relationships with the aging: honor of parents, respect for the old, activity over disengagement, the instrumentality of institutions, and obligation to respond to special needs (physical, material, socio-psychological, and spiritual).

274. Olitzky, K. M. (Ed.). (1991, Summer). Bernard Warach and JASA (The Jewish Association for Services for the Aged) [Special issue]. The Journal of Aging and Judaism, 5

This issue is dedicated to Bernard Warach on the occasion of his retirement. It contains six articles by Bernard Warach ranging from "The Social Services Block Grant and its Impact on Services to the Elderly" to "Filial Responsibility in the Care of the Aged: An Overview." The volume is witness to the ways in which ethical behavior is integral to every conception of the proper relationship between religion, spirituality, public practice, and aging.

275. Oliver, D. B. (1988, Winter). Ethical considerations in wellness programs for the elderly. Quarterly Papers on Religion and Aging, 4(2), 1-8.

This article argues that while "wellness" programs for the elderly may be helpful, there are ethical questions to be considered: What constitutes wellness in the elderly? When does it begin? When does it end? "I am convinced that 'wellness programs' for the elderly cannot succeed unless caregivers can first get past the wrinkles to see the person" (p. 5).

276. Orr, J. B. (1975). Aging and moral identity. In F. Sherman (Ed.), American Society of Christian Ethics: Selected papers from the 16th annual meeting (pp. 15-25). Knoxville, TN: American Society of Christian Ethics, and Scholars Press.

The author sees the possibility that society's need for disengagement of the elderly may lead the elderly to regress to earlier stages of moral judgment and perception. "Narcissism--the preoccupation with the self, with one's own opinions, with the body, with isolation and loneliness--is the threat, the extreme case, the terrible possibility of old age, its frightening prospects more real than the possibilities of achieving important forms of elderly wisdom" (p. 23). "The emotionally-electric experiences of growing old, of course, do not necessarily drive the elderly to narcissistic patterns of moral judgment. They merely constitute the temptation and the condition for such a change" (p. 24).

277. Spielman, B. J. (1988). On developing a geriatric ethic: Personhood in the thought of Stanley Hauerwas. Journal of Religion & Aging, 5(1/2), 23-33.

Healthcare providers are confronted by a variety of ethical problems, discussion of which has little persuasive power because it lacks an appropriate theoretical grounding. The author grounds geriatric ethics in the theory of the person described by Stanley Hauerwas, using his emphasis on the attributes of temporality, sociality, and limitation. Three ethical principles provide a framework for beginning to resolve ethical problems in geriatrics (such as paternalism, withdrawal of life-support, allocation of scarce resources). The ethical principles are continuity (which is concerned with the unity of one's life), interdependence (which seeks an appropriate level of support and care), and normality (which views aging as a normal part of the life course).

278. Spielman, B. J. (1986, Summer). Rethinking paradigms in geriatric ethics. Journal of Religion and Health, 25(2), 142-148.

This article questions the limits and appropriateness of autonomy (which has dominated medical ethics) as a starting point in developing a geriatric ethic. Described as qualities to be added are sociality (family and community relationships and responsibility), temporality (which recognizes limits), and embodiment (which respects our bodily nature).

279. Zlotowitz, B. M. (1986, Fall/Winter). Should intermarriage be performed for the elderly? Should one perform a marriage for an elderly couple who do not have a state license? The Journal of Aging and Judaism, 1, 68-69.

The author answers the first question by quoting from a resolution adopted by The Central Conference of American Rabbis that states that mixed marriage at any age should be discouraged. In the second question where the underlying reason for the request is often that the elderly do not want to lose their individual social security benefits but do not want to live together without benefit of marriage by clergy, the author concludes that the law of the land is supreme in this matter. It is therefore, a violation of Jewish law to violate the state law.

Dissertations

280. Sorenson, A. D. (1986). Family ethics and the aging family member (Unpublished Doctor of Ministry thesis, Garrett-Evangelical Theological Seminary).

The goals of the five workshops of this project were to educate participants on issues of aging, care options, and a process of ethical decision-making. It involved pre- and post-assessment of participants' cognitive learnings.

ETHICS IN THE PUBLIC DOMAIN

Books

281. Chenoweth, O. B. (1965). How senior citizens can save our country: A call to Christian, patriotic action. New York: Exposition, 82p.

"The unsound, uneconomic financial condition of our country today, manifest in our constantly increasing debt, makes me feel that it is up to our Senior Citizens, if they can be properly organized, to help our country find its way out of this chaotic ravine and onto a plain path of common sense. My aim is to lift the unwarranted burden of heavy tax bills now born by our senior citizens" (p. 16). This book is a vigorous denunciation of anything which is even remotely connected with New Deal politics or tainted by the "Red" meanace.

282. Glasse, L., & Hendricks, J. (1990, Summer). Gender and aging. Generations, 14(3).

These essays inquire about the difference gender makes in how people age. Articles consider: the importance of social expectations attached to gender; the reality that the problems of the very old may actually result from problems of gender and age; gender differences in physical and mental health, sexuality, care giving roles, minority elderly, the labor market, and public policy.

283. Hudson, R. B. (1984, Fall). The politics of aging. Generations, 9(1).

This issue considers: the new politics of aging which raises questions about the allocation of benefits for older persons; the curbing of Medicare costs; the high cost of long term care; the politics and policies of elderly housing; the potential influence of older people as a group on politics; and the future of advocay through the aging network (Leadership Council of Aging organizations).

284. Lerner, M. J. (1980). The belief in a just world. In M. J. Lerner, Belief in a just world: A fundamental delusion (pp. 9-30). New York: Plenum.

In this work in social psychology the author demonstrates a fundamental delusion which permeates our society, namely that people get what they deserve. "Commonly held negative stereotypes of minority-group members as diminished in personal worth, harmdoers, norm violaters qualify them for diminished access to desired resources, and often punishment in the guise of retribution for past or future 'crimes' to the society" (p. 16). This book was judged of such significance that it was awarded a quinquennial prize in religious psychology. Its relevance for aging is that the poor, frail, and female old are perceived stereotypically as minority-group members who are getting what they deserve.

285. Wiener, J. M. (Ed.).   (1990, Spring).   Long-term care financing. Generations, 14(2).

Essays on the continuing debate over who should pay for long-term care financing (the government or the individual) focus on public and private long-term care insurance, program design and cost of public and private insurance plans, and the inadequacy of programs for people with Alzheimer's and related dementing disorders.

Articles

286. Cole, T. (1988, October). The specter of old age: History, politics and culture in an aging America. Tikkun: A Bimonthly Jewish Critique of Politics, Culture & Society, 3, 14-18, 93-95.

In light of growing numbers of the old, old age becomes infused with ideological and political meaning in issues of generational equity. The discussion of payment for health care is located in notions of the moral economy of the life course--itself lodged in a view of the natural order now under seige. Solutions may be found in views of old age in which people see themselves not as fated creatures (life course) but as active beings who can solve life's problems (life-span approach to human development).

287. Collopy, B. J. (1985, Spring). Medicare: Ethical issues in public policy for the elderly. Social Thought, 11(2), 5-14.

One of four articles (Collopy, Curran, McCullough, Ryle) in a special issue of Social Thought on Ethics and Aging, this article identifies Medicare as more than an economic issue and locates the conversation about Medicare in the ethical realm.   Careful analysis reveals the existence of a distributive justice stand-off (merit vs. need) rooted in Medicare's largely blurred distributive presuppositions.   Included in this issue of studies by the National Conference of Catholic Charities Commission on Aging are responses of participants.

288. Eenigenburg, E. M.   (1983, Spring).   Ethical dynamics for the aging. Reformed Review, 36, 130-137.

Taking guidance from the general rule of geriatric ethics that losses should not be compounded, the author considers ethical issues involved in the care of the frail old: justice in the distribution of health-care resources and the use of high-technology anti-aging techniques.   The second section consists of the author's observation concerning the ability of aging persons to show moral change and growth.

289. Isaacs, L. W.   (1986, Fall/Winter).   With our young and with our old. The Journal of Aging and Judaism, 1, 57-67.

This article reports research on the development of ageist attitudes in young children.   Important variables include the role of the older adult as caregiver and not simply as social visitor.   Pre-school children should have frequent contact with older adults in significant roles. Authors of Jewish texts and other materials should be encouraged to portray elders in a vital and realistic manner. Intergenerational programs bring children and elders together to work toward common goals.

290. Kaplan, K. M., Sheskin, I. M., & Longino, C. F.   (1989, Winter). Conflicting images of elderly Jews: The larger picture. The Journal of Aging and Judaism, 4, 119-129.

This article places the care of the aged within the context of a larger social picture where the assets of the aging market are being targeted and attention is diverted from the needs of low-income elderly.

291. Larue, G. A.   (1976).   Religion and the aged.   In Irene Burnside (Ed.), Nursing and the aged (pp. 573-583).   New York: McGraw Hill.

The focus of this article is the way in which religious concepts affect patterns of life, living, mind-sets, and attitudes.   The author considers fate ("the good die young"), retirement, the beauty of age, and possibilities for a new ethic.

292. Linzer, N. (1987, Winter). Cross-currents in aging: Public policy and the Jewish response. The Journal of Aging and Judaism, 2, 78-83.

The author applies Levy's categorization of professional values to recent policies of the federal government toward the aged, and demonstrates how government values and Jewish values are in conflict. He argues that the duty of the Jewish professional is to lobby and protest against policies that demean and foster the helplessness of the sick aged.

293. McCullough, L. B. (1985, Spring). Long-term care for the elderly: An ethical analysis. Social Thought, 11(2), 40-52.

One of four articles (Collopy, Curran, McCullough, Ryle) in this issue of Social Thought on Ethics and Aging, the author raises the question of whether it is morally obligatory (and not simply 'humanitarian') for our society to assume the economic burden of a particular long-term care policy. The author uses an analysis of justice, respect for autonomy, and beneficence. His argument draws largely on secular ethic theory and only tangentially on moral theology. Included in this issue of studies by the National Conference of Catholic Charities Commission on Aging are responses of participants.

294. Meiburg, A. L. (1981, November 11). Conference on aging: Realistic expectations. The Christian Century, 98, 1151-1152.

This appeal to the religious community to muster its will to exercise responsibility for influencing social policy is occasioned by the then forthcoming White House Conference on Aging.

295. Parsons, T. (1974). Religion in postindustrial America: The problem of secularization. Social Research, 41, 193-225.

Although not specifically related to aging, this article introduces notions that may be important in the attempted development of a new acceptance of the old in society (or of the old by themselves). "[S]ome transcending of the consideration of erotic pleasure in defining the mediation and bonding of solidarity is a fundamental functional imperative for large communities" (p. 216). This attitude or affect has to do with the bond of solidarity between individuals and as members of a collective entity and is best described as a "secular" spiritual solidarity. This must be "institutionalized individualism" if it is to persist and must have an adequate rational component. "In the pattern of institutionalized individualism the keynote is [...] a much broader conception of the self-fulfillment of the individual in a social setting in which the aspect of solidarity [...] figures at least as prominently as does that of self-interest in the utilitarian sense" (p. 223).

296. Payne, B. P. (1986, Fall/Winter). Sex and the elderly: No laughing matter in religion. Journal of Religion & Aging, 3(1/2), 141-152.

This article examines sex, gender, and sexuality in relation to religious beliefs and aging. Five trends related to sex, aging, and the church/synagogue are discussed: from youth to adult congregation, from male to female congregations, from married to single, from either/or to multiple choice, and from exclusive to inclusive.

297. Peaston, M. (1984, Fall). Aspects of the person: Some themes in the recent writings of Paul Tournier. Pastoral Psychology, 33(1), 35-43.

This article locates the themes of Tournier's well-known Learning to grow old in the context of the whole corpus of his writings. Themes include aging as a new and necessary stage of life, second careers, possibility of growth, the moral climate of society and its interaction with the old, the attitude of the aged to their condition, and a healthy realism about death.

298. Ryle, E. J. (1985, Spring). The aging, income support programs, and economic well-being: A Catholic perspective. Social Thought, 11(2), 15-26.

One of four articles (Collopy, Curran, McCullough, Ryle) in a special issue of Social Thought on Ethics and Aging, the author identifies as most helpful contribution of Catholic Social thought to policy makers the "preferential option for the poor." The basic sustenance needs of the poor "must take precedence over lesser needs and rights of the middle and upper classes." [In a situation of budgetary crisis] the question of age vs. need would have to be answered by giving priority to need" (p. 25). Included in this issue of studies by the National Conference of Catholic Charities Commission on Aging are responses of participants.

299. Sample, T. (1986). The elderly poor, the future, and the church. Journal of Religion & Aging, 3(1/2), 121-139.

The author projects that demographic, economic and political trends in the United States may result in an ominous future for persons now 20 to 65 years of age. He sees the church becoming involved in at least four key roles (interpretative, advocacy, organizing, and building alternative institutions) to meet the economic and political challenges of the aging.

300. Sapp, S. (1991). Ethical issues in intergenerational equity. Journal of Religious Gerontology, 7(4), 1-15.

Any discussion of intergenerational equity must address value questions as well as matters of fact. This article suggests a way beyond the impasse created by the approach of "quandary ethics" (which asks what we can do to resolve the dilemma). The author suggests an ethic of virtue which asks who should we be in order to have the kind of society we want. Special attention is given to the notion of "civic virtue," historically and biblically.

301. Simmons, H. C. (1991). Ethical perspective on church and synagogue as intergenerational support system. Journal of Religious Gerontology, 7(4), 17-28.

This essay inquires as to why and on what basis religious groups do undertake or should undertake care of each other across generations. Five common-sensical reasons are examined, each of which is found to have merit and precedent and to be flawed and dangerous. Also examined is the implication for intergenerational care of an understanding of family/church as ideological abstraction, romantic image, place of treatment, last resort, process, and network. This inquiry helps understand motivation for participation of congregants in intergenerational support as congregations seek to engage people in intergenerational ministries.

302. Tobriner, A. (1985). Honor for old age: Sixteenth-Century pious ideal or grim delusion? Journal of Religion & Aging, 1(3), 1-21.

Pious writings from 16th century Tudor England are examined to seek insight into attitudes toward the elderly. Literature tends to indicate that although the old were publicly acknowledged in churches and meeting houses, veneration of the old was probably more fiction than fact. Tobriner continues her study of

16th century Tudor England with "Almshouses in Sixteenth-Century England: Housing for the Poor Elderly" in number 4 of this same volume. Contrary to the American experience with "poor houses" these English almshouses were and are "a humane solution to housing for non-wealthy elderly, all this within a framework guarded by centuries of precendents and legal guarantees" (p. 37).

303. Wood, D. (1979, October 3). Aging: A series of rebirths. The Christian Century, 96, 941-943.

The author, who just turned 30, finds it painful that our overly youth-conscious society "conveys the message that one's 30th birthday is the beginning of the end and that one's 65th birthday renders one economically useless" (p. 941). He implores churches to help in challenging the idolization of youth and in changing discriminatory attitudes and practices against the old.

Dissertations

304. Loetterle, B. C. (1984). Ageless prose: A study of the media projected images of aging as reflected in content analysis of magazines for older persons (Doctor of Philosophy dissertation, City University of New York). DAI, 45, 2220A.

This dissertation is based on a content analysis of Modern Maturity and 50 Plus. Principal categories of analysis include: leisure time, realities of aging, retirement, value orientation, religion and spirituality, daily living, careers, and volunteer activity. The data indicate that there has been continuity in editorial direction of these magazines over the twenty years studied. These magazines have taken on the task of socializing the healthy elderly into a view of age as a victory and as a time of growth and fulfillment.

FILIAL RESPONSIBILITY

Books

305. Anderson, M. J. (1979). Your aging parents. St. Louis, MO: Concordia, 126p.

This book is for children of aging parents who will soon face decisions determing the course of future events for both generations. The author helps the reader explore important issues, offering sound, practical Christian advice on how to best help one's aging parents. Topics include feelings of guilt and obligation, who is your parents' keeper, home versus institutional care, and where to find professional help.

306. Bucchieri, T. F. (1975). Keep your old folks at home. Canfield, OH: Alba, 171p.

This is an account of how a retired professional woman shared her life and her home with a senile aunt, caring for the physical and emotional needs of a disoriented woman in her eighties. Readers may join the author in her condemnation of the way in which American society cares for the senile; some may be encouraged to imitate her decision and be helped by her "life-tested" advice.

307. Deane, B. (1989). Caring for your aging parents: When love is not enough. Colorado Springs, CO: Navpress, 276p.

This is a comprehensive guide from a Christian perspective for the many challenges of caring for an aging parent. The first few chapters emphasize the relationship of the adult child's emotional and spiritual needs to those of the elderly parent: love, healing, honest communications, understanding and forgiveness. Additional chapters present practical issues: housing, medical and legal decisions. The last chapter returns to emotional concerns--helping a dying parent.

308. DuFresne, F. (1985). Home care: An alternate to the nursing home. Elgin, IL: Bretheren Press, 127p.

This book offers straightforward, practical information on the particulars of home nursing care, which is according to the author, an adventure in love. Emotional as well as physical needs of caregivers are considered as the author quietly tells the story at the end of the book of caring for her husband at home.

309. Fritz, D. B. (1972). Growing old is a family affair. Richmond, VA: John Knox, 96p.

A common-sensical and inspirational book writen by a 70 year old. The book's theme (not developed in any depth) is that attitudes toward aging and the aged, preparation for later years, and the actual experience of them happen in or are related to families.

310. Gillies, J. (1988). Care giving. Wheaton, IL: Harold Shaw, 212p.

This book is an account of experiences the author and his wife shared for eleven years as caregivers of their parents. It offers practical advice to those caring for aging loved ones on matters such as personal hygiene and grooming, nutrition, exercise, activities, money and the law, communication, and funeral arrangements.

311. Gillies, J. (1985). A guide to compassionate care of the aging. Nashville, TN: Thomas Nelson, 225p.

The author, using his professional experience and his experience as a caregiver, has compiled a practical guide of program options to support caregivers. The book is organized along Maslow's hierarchy of needs: physiological, security, emotional, esteem, and personal growth. Also included is a potpourri of ideas for innovators and an appendix with a community survey form, menus and recipes, adult day care federal funding sources, and agency addresses.

312. Jensen, M. D. (1985). Your aging parent. Grand Rapids, MI: Zondervan, 124p.

Practical solutions suggested may enable adults to cope with or obtain help for aging parents so that the commandment to honor our parents can be kept.

313. Lester, A. D., & Lester, J. L. (1980). Understanding aging parents. Philadelphia, PA: Westminster Press, 120p.

This book discusses the special relationship between mid-life adults and their aging parents. The authors offer practical advice based on how others have struggled and coped with the problems of aging.

314. Pierskalla, C. S., & Heald, J. D. (1988). Help for families of the aging: Caregivers can express love and set limits. Swarthmore, PA: Support Source, 144p.

This leader manual includes a 78-page participant workbook for an eight-week seminar for relatives of the frail elderly. Sessions address adjusting to aging, learning to listen, problem solving, helping a friend, coping with feelings, and caregiving alternatives. The workbook (which can be purchased separately)contains pencil exercises, diagrams, readings, skits, monologues, and discussion questions.

315. Pillari, V. (1986). Pathways to family myths. New York: Brunner/Mazel, 188p.

This study identifies various types of family myths: harmony, family scapegoat, catastrophism, pseudomutuality, overgeneralization, togetherness, salvation and redemption. As these myths tend to endure and to function into old age and in the relationships of generations, some of the far-reaching and persistent power of these myths may affect decisions of filial care and responsibility.

316. Smith, H. I. (1987). You and your parents: Strategies for building an adult relationship. Minneapolis, MN: Augsburg, 157p.

This "how to" book for adult children uses scripture in presenting 10 guidelines for building a positive parental relationship. The author presents ways to recognize five fears that influence relationships with parents: fear of change, rejection, success, illness, and loss of dignity.

317. Zarit, S. N., & Sommers, T. (1985, Fall). Caregivers. Generations, 10(1).

The focus of this issue is on understanding caregivers and their problems. Essays discuss the necessity of tailoring interventions to meet the unique needs of caregivers, gender differences in caregiving, care in minority families, stories from three caregivers, implications for caregivers of elder abuse laws, deciding to institutionalize an elder, and the importance of forming self-help groups around an identifiable issue rather than caregiving in general.

Articles

318. Chernick, M. (1987, Spring/Summer). Who pays? The Talmudic approach to filial responsibility. The Journal of Aging and Judaism, 1, 109-117.

The author notes that the relationship of parents and adult children is complicated. Using an analysis of the text (Tractate Kiddusin 31b-32a) the author derives concrete principles for action. He notes the prevailing rabbinic view that a parent should pay for the physical elements of his or her honor. He also notes that the relationship of adult child to diminished parent cannot become one of inverted roles and that the lives of the adult children "cannot be swallowed up by the crushing of their individuality under impossible burdens created by parents" (p. 116).

319. Curran, C. E. (1985, Spring). Filial responsibility for an elderly parent. Social Thought, 11(2), 27-39.

One of four articles (Collopy, Curran, McCullough, Ryle) in this issue of Social Thought on Ethics and Aging, the author, arguing from the Catholic tradition of destributive justice, claims that more should be done for the elderly and that the state must assume much of the burden. Addressing questions of cost he states that "the tax burden should depend on one's ability to pay, with those having more being required to pay more" (p. 38). Included in this issue of studies by the National Conference of Catholic Charities Commission on Aging are responses of participants.

320. Dantzer, K. S. (Ed.). (1980, May 2). Demands of an aging population: Family solutions. Christianity Today, 24, 12-13.

This editorial reminds evangelical Christians that abandoning elderly family members because taking care of them would reduce living standards is--according to biblical teaching--equated with unbelief. The faith demands that families provide for their elders.

321. De La Motta, J. (1990, Winter). Honour the aged. The Journal of Aging and Judaism, 5, 147-153.

This partial text of an address delivered in Charleston, SC in June 1843 traces the history of filial duty--"that which nothing can obtain for us more effectually prolonged years, happiness, and prosperity" (p. 149).

322. Elliot, E. (1988, July 15). Forget-me-not. Christianity Today, 32, 22-23.

This essay is a reflection on God's love for the elderly mother of the author who lives in a nursing home because she requires more care than family members could give her. Her mother's story illustrates the importance of continuing to love and care for family members with impaired mental capacities. The story is available as a little paper-back book with illustrations (Forget me not: Elliot, E. (1989). Loving God's Aging Children. Portland, OR: Multnomah).

323. Guttmann, D. (1990, Spring). Filial responsibility--A logotherapeutic view. The Journal of Aging and Judaism, 4, 161-180.

The author explores the obligations of adult children toward their aged parents from traditional Jewish sources and from logotheraphy. He recognizes the possible stress arising from the obligation to filial responsibility but notes that from a logotherapeutic perspective there are wonderful opportunities to fill life with meaning and thus meet the most important noetic or spiritual need of a human being. He distinguishes between obligations that arise out of freedom and responsibility and obligations that arise out of demands by authority.

324. Johnson, P. T., & Van Meter, M. J. (1985, Spring). Family decision making, long-term care for the elderly, and the role of religious organizations: Part I: The issues and the challenge. Journal of Religion & Aging, 1(3), 61-69.

This is the first of three articles focusing on family decision making and long-term care arrangements for frail elderly. (Part II: A review, and Part III: Interventions for religious professionals and organizations, appear in Summer 1985, 1(4). Part I presents facts indicating that contrary to popular myths families today give their elderly members physical, emotional, social, and economic support. However, because people are living longer and more women are part of the labor force, middle aged persons with elderly parents need support and education in order to make the best long-term care decisions. Part II reviews selected literature indicating that adult children suffer stress from caregiving and guilt from institutionalizing a parent. Part III discusses interventions that clergy and other religious professionals and organizations can provide such as counseling, resource files of community services, and education/support groups.

325. Linzer, N. (1986, Fall/Winter). The obligations of adult children to aged parents: A view from Jewish tradition. The Journal of Aging and Judaism, 1,

34-48.

This article delineates the moral obligations of adult children to their aging parents from Judaic, ethical, and mental health perspectives. Similarities and differences are noted. The article considers honor and reverence, obligations for financial support, moral obligations to elderly parents, parents as friends, dependency as a moral claim, the "sandwich" generation, obligations of sons and daughters in Judaism, and limitations of filial responsibility (the sick parent).

326. Meier, L. (1977, Fall). Filial responsibility to the senile parent: A Jewish approach. Journal of Psychology and Judaism, 2, 45-53.

Filial responsibility towards senile parents is explored by an analysis of Talmudic anecdotes as interpreted by Maimonides. Although filial responsibility never terminates, limitations to filial endurance in the case of a chronic brain syndrome are recognized. Even in such a case, however, the adult child must delegate the care of the parent to others. A temporary situation, such as an acute brain syndrome, does not alter the obligation of filial responsibility.

327. Mickelsen, A. (1981). To honor your parents: The chance for a lifetime. Christianity Today, 25, 791-795.

This article states biblical teachings that admonish Christians to take care of their aging parents; however, how we honor our parents "is an intensely personal matter to be worked out between the parents and adult children. . ." (p. 795). Care must be taken to avoid abuse, not only in its violent forms, but in the form of gaining control of parental assets, treating parents like children, leaving parents out of family and church activities, or leaving their care up to only one of several adult children.

328. Oliver, D. B. (1986, Fall/Winter). The real nursing home scandal: Will it get worse in the future? Journal of Religion & Aging, 3(1/2), 153-163.

The author argues that the blame for poor quality nursing home care is misplaced. The religious sector has abandoned those who live in nursing homes. The church/synagogue should become the extended family for disconnected and isolated older persons, particularly for those living in nursing homes.

329. Post, S. G. (1989). Filial morality in an aging society. Journal of Religion & Aging, 5(4), 15-29.

An inquiry into what adult children owe their elderly parents, this article defends filial obligation as rooted in the Judeo-Christian moral heritage. While children may find themselves with heavier burdens than anticipated and may be tempted to unravel the traditional arguments affirming filial obligations, the author rejects any such shift in moral consciousness.

330. Sapp, S. (1984, Winter). On our obligations to the elderly. Journal of Religion & Aging, 1(2), 27-37.

Sapp advocates that one way to break the chain of death denial in our society is to keep the elderly within their family during their final years. The Judeo-Christian moral tradition of putting others before self supports this approach even though keeping the elderly in the family may create inconvenience for adult children.

331. Stendahl, B. (1979, November 14:). Honor your father and your mother. The Christian Century, 96, pp. 1119-1124.

Based on a chapter from Stendahl's book Sabattical which is structured upon the Ten Commandments, this article deals with the author's perceptions of her aging parents.

Dissertations

332. Christiansen, A. J. (1982/1983). Autonomy and dependence in old age: An ethical analysis (Doctor of Philosophy dissertation, Yale University). DAI, 43, 3940A.

This study explores the moral rationality of familial dependence in old age. It proposes a set of moral beliefs and basic attitudes which account for filial responsibility and parental trust while taking into account the risk of dependence. Human dignity, based on the desire of persons for mutual recognition, is the justification for familial dependence. The values of autonomy, family membership, and welfare are examined and are connected to the dignity of the aged. Also studied are the limits of moral reasoning in this area and the religious implications of these limits.

333. Goist, D. F. (1980). "Will you still need me? Will you still feed me? When I'm 84" (Doctor of Philosophy dissertation, Case Western Reserve University). DAI, 41, 1119A.

This anthropological study of two groups of elderly Jews examines differences in their willingness to ask for help from their children and in self-image and level of anxiety. Factors studied include the quality of earlier relationships within family of orientation, shared lifestyles of aged parents and adult children, and the presence of life-long intimate friends.

334. Krentel, D. P. (1986). The care of the geriatric mentally retarded (Doctor of Ministry thesis, Dallas Theological Seminary). DAI, 48, 225A.

This descriptive study argues from a biblical perspective that the siblings of the geriatric mentally retarded bear special responsibility for their care and treatment. Also provided is a financial model to help a 'typical' family accumulate enough resources to provide quality care for the mentally retarded family member.

335. Stueve, C. A. (1985). What's to be done about mom and dad? Daughters' relations with elderly parents (Doctor of Philosophy dissertation, University of California, Berkeley). DAI, 47, 1023A.

This dissertation studies adult daughters' interactions with their elderly parents and the daughters' conceptions of filial responsibility. Significant predictors of involvement included physical closeness, poor health of parents, and no full-time employment on the part of the daughter. The women's social class, ethnicity, and religious affiliation were important. Those who acknowledged extensive filial obligations tended to be close to their ethnic origins, Catholic, and working-class.

TERMINATION OF LIFE

Books

336. Spring, B., & Larson, E. (1988). Euthanasia: Spiritual, medical and legal issues in terminal health care. Portland, OR: Multnomah, 219p.

A discussion of the complex and controversial issue of euthanasia written from a Christian perspective. While the book opposes euthanasia itself, it presents a balanced view of this important issue.

Articles

337. Cohn, E. P. (1986, Fall/Winter). Suicide among the elderly: The religious response. Journal of Religion & Aging, 3(1/2), 165-179.

This article examines recent findings about the incidence and reasons for suicide, studies the Judeo-Christian tradition about suicide, and inquires what steps will need to be taken if the religious community is to respond appropriately to suicide among the elderly. It concludes with an examination of the religious agenda for the future in regard to the phenomenon of suicide among the elderly. People considering suicide will turn increasingly to the religious community for life affirmation.

338. Donow, H. S. (1989). Religion and science: The Wandering Jew and Methuselah. Journal of Aging Studies, 3, 67-73.

The legend of the Wandering Jew dramatizes the theme that longevity is a curse. This Jewish perspective is consistent with a Christian perspective which traditionally saw the goal of life to die and be with God. Both stand in contrast to a scientific view which finds in Methuselah a symbol of the scientific quest for long life. The author discusses several twentieth-century writers whose characters overcome the aging process with the help of science. The authors are ambivalent about longevity.

339. Feldman, L. J. (1989, Summer). A Halakhic/ethical view of withdrawing feeding and hydration. The Journal of Aging and Judaism, 3, 191-198.

Based on the threefold sanctity of life (it is untouchable by others, it is an absolute and not relative to anyone, and no person has to apologize for being alive, whatever his or her condition) Jews are called to resist trends toward withdrawing nutrition and hydration.

340. Gruman, G. J. (1973). An historical introduction to ideas about voluntary euthanasia: With a bibliographic survey and guide for interdisciplinary studies. Omega, 4(2), 87-138.

This lengthy article examines the evolution of modern ideas about euthanasia through renaissance humanism, the Reformation and the mercantilist ethic, the Enlightenment, the Nineteenth Century, and the Twentieth Century.

341. Hughes, R. (1988). Ethical problems in living will legislation. Journal of Religion & Aging, 5(1/2), 35-50.

This article examines a particular piece of legislation concerning the living will. In that context, four ethical problems in living wills are identified: 1) the problem of competence, 2) the confusion of medical means (ordinary, extraordinary), 3) the problem of liability, and 4) the ambiguity of the right to die. The author concludes that churches can facilitate social change by insisting on ethically responsible legislation.

342. Kravitz, L. S. (1987, Spring/Summer). Who shall live and who shall die? The Journal of Aging and Judaism, 1, 118-125.

The author deals with a variety of specific situations each of which requires an individual response.

343. Miles, S. H., & August, A. (1990, Spring/Summer). Courts, gender, and "The right to die". Law, Medicine & Health Care, 18(1-2), 85-95.

This article examines judicial reasoning about women's and men's right to die, specifically as it takes into account evidence of men's preferences with regard to life-sustaining treatment while rejecting such evidence for women.

344. Sherwin, B. L. (1987, Fall). Euthanasia: A Jewish view. The Journal of Aging and Judaism, 2, 35-57.

This study discusses Jewish writings on attempts to resolve inevitable conflicts that arise in the challenges and crises at the end of life. In particular there is an inevitable conflict between a commitment to the value of life and a commitment to lessen pain and suffering during the process of dying. The author gives insights from the Jewish tradition but also outlines a position that would justify active euthanasia in certain cases.

345. Sittler, J. (1986). Reflections on aging. Second Opinion: Health, Faith

and Ethics, 3, 126-132.

At age 82 a prominent theologian raises important ethical issues which take on new meaning and urgency in our present situation. His principal reflections are on suicide. Wisdom on the wrongness of suicide is completely irrelevant to many of the realities of the current world. "Instead of making an ethical judgment in the presence of certifiable facts, I had to make a judgment in the midst of indeterminancy. That is becoming the situation we all must face with the care of the aging" (p. 129-30). Other issues are the lack of attention paid to the views of the aging themselves and the role of religious institutions in this era of extended life.

346. Zlotowitz, B. (1989, Summer). Does an elderly patient have the right to refuse dialysis? The Journal of Aging and Judaism, 3, 211-213.

The author argues that in order to reconcile Halacha (the person is the final arbiter of medical treatment) and the law of the land, a person should write a Living Will indicating what life-sustaining measures are not wanted. A contrary opinion is offered by Dayle Friedman in this journal, 4(4).

Dissertations

347. Kuepper, S. L. (1981). Euthanasia in America, 1890-1960: The controversy, the movement, and the law (Doctor of Philosophy dissertation, Rutgers University). DAI, 42, 1761A.

This study examines cultural developments from 1890-1960 which gave rise to the concern over euthanasia and helped shape that concern: pro-sucide arguments influenced by relativist ethics following Darwinism, a growing concern about chronic and degenerative diseases, the advocacy of involuntary euthanasia, and so on. The study concludes that the current discussion of euthanasia, in the context of a bio-technological revolution, is conditioned by the manner in which the pre-1960 issues were discussed.

348. Montgomery, L. R. (1984). The ethical imperatives which emerge from a theological perspective on disintegration at the end of life (Doctor of Philosophy dissertation, Rice University). DAI, 46, 1651A.

This dissertation studies disintegration at the end of life which requires additional care or help if people are to be able to stay in their own homes. The

Judeo-Christian mandate to care for one another (regardless of condition) is invoked to argue for reconciliation as homecoming, a term which has both a this world and a transcendent significance. The author identifies home as the site where the very old are best cared for and argues that the economic sphere ought to serve the family. Institutions, the place of last resort, ought to be modelled on the family home.

RIGHT WAYS TO BE AN OLDER ADULT: AUTHOR IDENTIFIED AS A SENIOR

Books

349. Abernethy, J. B. (1975). <u>Old is not a four-letter word!</u> Nashville, TN: Abingdon, 159p.

This positive, hopeful book by a retired lecturer on human relations addresses two basic questions: How does a person maintain a sense of worth, given society's negative attitudes towards aging? What does an individual need to learn for the later years of life?

350. Anderson, C. M. (1971). <u>Don't put on your slippers yet</u>. Grand Rapids, MI: Zondervan, 120p.

Along with inspirational thoughts, the author provides practical advice on practical issues of age--reduced budget, loss of mate, bigger medical bills, contributing to the lives of others.

351. Andrews, E. M. (1968). <u>Facing and fulfilling the later years</u>. Wallingford, PA: Pendle Hill, 31p.

This personal reflection on the later years is informed, in part, by the years the author spent in the training of those concerned with the welfare of the elderly.

352. Arnold, O. (1976). <u>Guide yourself through old age</u>. Philadelphia, PA: Fortress, 116p.

The purpose of this book is to relieve worry about old age by straight talk and common-sense counsel from a man living in a retirement community. Concerns discussed are housing, finances, health, and personality.

353. Asquith, G. H. (1975). Living creatively as an older adult: Practical suggestions for getting the most out of life. Scottdale, PA: Herald, 178p.

Writing at age 70 the author is able to create an empathy in the reader for the inner world view of the older person as person. His premise is that as in other periods of life, there is a balance between good and bad. Asquith works this out in chapters on physical stamina, friends and neighbors, money, recreation, educational opportunities, the healthy mind, and spiritual strength.

354. Dye, H. E. (1979). The touch of friendship. Nashville, TN: Broadman, 144p.

The author, a retired Southern Baptist minister, wrote this book for one reason: "to cause the reader (and the writer) to reach out to others; to continue to be a part of the stream of life; to come out of our shells, or not to retire within them; to make and to be friends" (p. 19). The stories in this book reveal the value of having Christian friends especially in the senior years.

355. Hutchison, F. (1991). Aging comes of age: Older people finding themselves. Louisville, KY: Westminster/John Knox, 112p.

This is a "why to" book by an 80-year-old retired minister who writes full-time about aging. He encourages older people to have satisfying personal lives while contributing to society.

356. Jacob, N. (1981). Growing old: A view from within. Wallingford, PA: Pendle Hill, 31p.

This little work (Pendle Hill Pamphlet 239) is a testimony of a retired social worker. She speaks of loss, diminishment, and death but also of riches: emotion recollected in tranquility, discovering the younger generation, learning to live in the present.

357. Maves, P. B. (1986). Faith for the older years: Making the most of life's second half. Minneapolis, MN: Augsburg, 189p.

This is a faith-filled guide to decision making and transitions in maturity. The author has been a researcher, practitioner, and minister in the field of aging for almost 40 years.

358. Maves, P. B. (1983). A place to live in your later years: Making decisions about housing alternatives. Minneapolis, MN: Augsburg, 127p.

This is a book to help retiring persons decide how and where to live by using problem solving skills derived from the Christian faith. Chapters include confronting change, coping with change, housing options, changing living arrangements, nursing care, and hospice.

359. Miller, E. F. (1976). How to grow older gracefully. Liguori, MO: Liguori Publications, 64p.

The author, a Redemptorist priest for 50 years, reflects on growing old for older readers facing problems of aging: loneliness, changes in family and lifestyle, and irritability.

360. Mow, A. B. (1969). So who's afraid of birthdays? Philadelphia, PA: J. B. Lippincott, 128p.

Written in the author's seventy-sixth year, this book is inspirational and common-sensical without being unrealistically upbeat. It has a clear religious and Christian focus.

361. Peachey, J. L. (Ed.). (1983, March/April). Bringing the lamps with you: An exploration of the adventure of growing older [Special issue]. Christian Living, 30(3-4).

Articles in this issue include: "They Sold My Grandmother's House Last Week;" "Honoring Your Father and Mother When Their Days Are Long;" "Teaching Children About Growing Old;" "Old Age is the Time to Practice What We've Preached."

362. Pearce, J. W. (1982). Ten good things I know about retirement. Nashville, TN: Broadman, 92p.

The ten good things described by a man now ten years retired are: pleasure, freedom, love, hobbies, work, friendship, children, reminiscing, chance, and God.

363. Purcell, W. (1982). The Christian in retirement. London: Mowbray, 119p.

The author's five steps for creative retirement are: don't live in the past, explore ways of making a new beginning, work towards making a fuller life, know your own physical and mental limitations, and look beyond this life.

364. Sanders, J. O. (1982). Your best years. Chicago, IL: Moody, 132p.

A positive, realistic, and inspirational book in 17 brief chapters, this work stresses an optimistic and cheerful outlook on old age in a society which gives this insufficient emphasis. The author states: "Realism and optimism with regard to the aging process can sleep in the same bed" (p. 8). The author, writing in his late seventies, demonstrates his own saying in a plain and thoughtful way.

365. Skoog, E. C. (1980). I'm retired--and I'm glad. Valley Forge, PA: Judson, 95p.

"This book is all about one person's thoughts and experiences leading up to and including the first year of that beautiful time of life called retirement" (p.7).

366. Tournier, P. (1971). Learn to grow old. New York: Harper & Row, 248p.

A book of personal counsel by a noted Swiss psychiatrist for those preparing to retire or already retired. The book concentrates on work and leisure, the need for a more humane society, the condition of the old, and aspects of Chrsitian faith. (This book has been reissued by Westminster/John Knox Press, Louisville, KY, 1991.).

Articles

367. Constance, Sister. (1982). Stuff of other men's lives. In P. Jefferson

(Ed.), Voice from the mountain: New life for the old law (pp. 54-64). Toronto, Canada: Anglican Book Centre.

In her 70s the author keeps reminding herself that "I am the stuff of both my ancestors and those who are coming after me, and this puts me in a fairly frightening position--having to live really responsibly, seeing myself molded into the stuff of other people's lives" (p. 54). It is the responsibility of the family to witness to the relationship of caring: for each other, for parents, for significant others, for all regardless of age, race, or gender.

368. Simcox, C. E. (1987, December 2). The gift of aging. The Christian Century, 104, 1090-1092.

This personal testimony of an elder is notable for a number of literary quotations.

369. Tournier, P. (1988). Lifestyles leading to physical, mental and social wellbeing in old age. Journal of Religion & Aging, 4(3/4), 13-26.

Writing as a well 87-year-old, the author comments on the need to remain as active as possible physically, mentally, and socially. He notes that old age is the fruit of the whole of existence and that every person is always preparing for his or her old age.

RIGHT WAYS TO BE AN OLDER ADULT: AUTHOR NOT IDENTIFIED AS A SENIOR

Books

370. Anderson, M. J. (1978). Looking ahead: The realities of aging: Face them with faith. St. Louis, MO: Concordia, 126p.

This inspirational and common-sensical approach to the realities of old age that bring changes in an individual's lifestyle considers where to live, financial worries, health, second careers, death and dying, and faith.

371. Arthur, J. K. (1969). Retire to action: A guide to voluntary service. Nashville, TN: Abingdon, 254p.

This comprehensive guide to retirement assumes that goals must include purposeful activity for happiness. The author explores a wide variety of opportunities for service in urban, small town, and rural areas, under a variety of auspices (national organizations, government, overseas service). Many of the specifics are dated but the thrust and organization of the book are still valid.

372. Biegert, J. E. (1982). So we're growing older. New York: Pilgrim, 24p.

This tiny inspirational pamphlet stresses the possession of a right attitude, flexibility, ego differentiation, body transcendence, ego transcendence, and a meaningful faith.

373. Frost, M. (n.d.). Making the most of your golden years. Cincinnati, OH: Standard, 96p.

This inspirational book introduces 17 senior citizens who have found ways to enjoy their golden years to the fullest. Each chapter concludes with several "points to consider." According to the author, the special challenges of maturity include the areas of health, finance, social life, mental stimulation, and goals.

374. Gaffney, M. (n.d.). Growing old. Chicago, IL: Claretian, 40p.

This common-sensical pamphlet discusses briefly the physical, psychological, practical, social, and religious dimensions of age.

375. Gager, D. (1987). It's my move: Older adults choose how to live. Nashville, TN: Discipleship Resources, 21p.

This brief companion guide to It's Your Move provides a resource for older adults, their family and friends, pastors, educators, and counselors. As a workbook or counseling tool, this guide can help older adults plan for their future housing needs.

376. Gager, D. (1987). It's your move: Older adults choose how to live. Nashville, TN: Discipleship Resources, 103p.

Clergy, older adults, counselors, and children of older adults can use this book and its companion It's My Move to look together at alternative housing arrangements and extended care. The pastor or counselor can use this guide to help an older adult or family with the medical, financial, social/emotional, environmental, and self-help concerns of older adults.

377. Geddes, J. (1987). The better half of life. Nashville, TN: Broadman, 192p.

According to Geddes, a clinical psychologist and minister, senior adults and workers with senior adults need to know about the new science of aging--a science that negates the second half of life as the twilight years and as a time when older people disengage from life. The book offers practical suggestions on developing realistic and positive Christian attitudes in the second half of life.

378. Howe, R. L. (1974). Live all your life. Waco, TX: Word, 168p.

Viewing life as a pilgrimage, this book stresses the now, creativity, giving of ourselves, acquiring new interests, and learning to love while growing older.

379. Howell, J. C. (1979). Senior adult family life: A source book. Nashville, TN: Broadman, 137p.

Written from a Christian perspective, this book discusses the variety of family lifestyles in which older adults may live, developmental patterns (physical, psychological, social, and spiritual), maturity as a continuing process, living with family crises, marital conflicts (including remarriage), and family conflicts (parent-child, sibling).

380. Hulme, W. E. (1986). Vintage years: Growing older with meaning and hope. Philadelphia, PA: Westminster, 120p.

Written by a professor of pastoral care and counseling at Luther Northwestern Theological Seminary, this book discusses the need for meaning in aging, how ageism shapes our own image of aging, problems and opportunities of aging, spiritual resources, and individual stories of older persons who have lived meaningful lives. Hulme emphasizes that quality aging begins when we are younger.

381. Janss, E. (1984). Making the second half the best half: How to plan now for making retirement the best part of your life. Minneapolis, MN: Bethany House, 192p.

Janss, a United Methodist minister, has written this guidebook for those in their fifties and sixties to read before retirement in order to be prepared mentally and emotionally for a positive and rewarding retirement. Each chapter includes study questions or exercises for personal study and/or group discussion.

382. Kipp, M. (1980). Living life to the fullest: Practical help for the senior years. Springfield, MO: Gospel Publishing House, 158p.

This large print resource book is designed to get the reader off to a good start in planning for retirement. The author shows the reader how to understand the aging process and then gives useful and practical ideas on adjusting to changes.

383. Lathrop, S. G. (1884). Fifty years and beyond; or gathered gems for the aged. Chicago, IL: F. H. Revell, 400p.

"This volume is a religious miscellany [published in 1884] for the mature and the aged. The author has sought to enrich its pages by such articles as will impart instruction and comfort to the aged, teaching how the later years of life may be spent, so that they shall constitute the happiest and most useful of all life's periods" (p.5). The range of articles is quite astounding; their content reveals a view of old age which has normative power to this day.

384. Mace, D., & Mace, V. (1985). Letters to a retired couple: Marriage in the later years. Valley Forge, PA: Judson, 160p.

The authors, pioneers in the marriage enrichment movement, wrote upbeat, personal letters offering common-sense helps to couples as they grow older. The letters address the crisis of retirement; health; sex and gender; commitment in marriage; communication; conflict resolution; relating to children and grandchildren; death, dying, and bereavement; faith in the divine purpose.

385. Madden, M. C., & Madden, M. B. (1980). For grandparents: Wonders and worries. Philadelphia, PA: Westminster, 118p.

This book, part of the Christian Care Books series, is written from the authors' experience as grandparents and from their training in pastoral counseling. The Madden's examine the grandparent-grandchild relationship from a positive and enthusiastic viewpoint, the feelings involved, the inner and outer life of the child, relating to grandchildren at different growth stages, grandparents and grandchildren living together, and the Foster Grandparent Program. This book could provide a basis for a study group.

386. Mandel, E. (1981). The art of aging. Minneapolis, MN: Winston, 132p.

This large print book is designed as a creative guide to living with zest, joy, and grace with information on nourishing body, mind, and spirit. It provides how-to-do-it steps on Yoga, meditation, acupressure, fasting, Tai Chi, and pain control; inspirational interviews with Maggie Kuhn, Norman Cousins, Carl Rogers, Elisabeth Kubler-Ross, and others.

387. Ortlund, R., & Ortlund, A. (1976). The best half of life. Glendale, CA: Regal, 125p.

Written by a couple as they turned 50, this book is a blend of inspiration and enthusiasm in its approach to the "next 25 years." The authors state that facing the second half of life is an exhilarating challenge.

388. Otte, E. (1974). Welcome Retirement. St Louis, MO: Concordia, 78p.

This book gives an inspirational and optimistic approach to retirement. The six-page chapter on "Your Spiritual Health" contributes nothing specific to the literature on the spiritual life of the retired person.

389. Schuckman, T. (1975). Aging is not for sissies. Philadelphia, PA: Westminster, 125p.

An inspirational and common-sensical approach to the last third of life, this affirmative book asks its reader to accept all of life, even growing old. Topics include health, finance, living accommodations, learning, and volunteering.

390. Smith, T. R. (1981). In favor of growing older: Guidelines and practical suggestions for planning your retirement career. Scottdale, PA:

Herald, 197p.

This practical retirement guide takes a positive and wholistic approach to the last third of life. The book has three foci: the material is written for all ages of adults; priority is given to helping persons to develop their resources throughout life; and help is given to recognize the resources and basic needs of the majority of older persons who are not institutionalized.

391. Whitman, V. (1967). Around the corner from sixty. Chicago, IL: Moody, 142p.

This book of essays is designed to challenge senior citizens "to believe that God's grace is always available and sufficient" (p. 7). It is upbeat, laced with scripture verses, and promotes the importance of remaining active in the later years through balance and busyness which results in contentment. It advocates volunteering, becoming active in civic affairs, reading, traveling, and attending college courses.

392. Wolf, B., & Wolf, U. (1977). Ten to get ready: Preparing for retirement. Philadelphia, PA: Parish Life, 96p.

This resource on preparing for retirement is written from a Christian perspective. It advocates planning for retirement a decade in advance and addresses issues such as health, housing and location, finances, life-style, job prospects, use of leisure time, wills and death. Information for organizing and conducting pre-retirement sessions is included. The coordinator's guidebook contains many helpful learning activities, but the participant reader is dated.

Articles

393. Bissonnette, W. S. (1919, July). On the new life at sixty. Methodist Review, 102, 599-604.

The author, writing at age 45, states that he has made a covenant, signed a bond: at "sixty all things will be made new. Body and spirit will rally to a new unity for that career. [...] At sixty a man may begin to live" (p. 604). He vigorously rejects the "last heresy" that the ravages of age are inevitable. Rather, aspiration will define the quality of life.

394. Drakeford, J. W. (1984, Winter). How growing old looks from within: A study of John Wesley's perception of the aging process as revealed in his journal's "Birthday Reflections". Journal of Religion & Aging, 1(2), 39-51.

Beginning at age 51 and continuing periodically until age 88, John Wesley wrote his "Birthday Reflections" in his diary. In this record of his aging experiences, Wesley noted factors he considered important to his successful aging: good diet, effective stress management, sense of purpose, activity, varied interests, and an optimistic attitude.

395. Grumpert, M. (1954, September). Old age and productive loss. Pastoral Psychology, 5, 37-44.

The author interviewed informally a number of statesmen, philosophers, scientists, artists, writers, and businessmen. All were of above-average intelligence and knowledge. He concluded that in spite of their physical limitations, these were successful old people--soft, tender, warm human beings, capable of enjoying life. "The human value of an individual may rise with his material decline. We must learn to discover or to rediscover human values as powerful and vital social agents of which our society is in bitter need" (p. 44).

396. Haskew, D. W. (1929, April). The art of growing older. The Methodist Quarterly Review, 78, 249-258.

This article is an inspirational and moralizing recommendation that people learn the art of growing older while they are still young in years. The characteristics of good aging are spelled out in detail: gratitude, cheerfulness, stored-up kindness, peacefulness in aging, a happy spirit. This article is a strong and uncritical statement about how to be attractive in old age.

397. Hunt, A. E. (1988, April). Seniors who make a difference. Fundamentalist Journal, 7, 33-35.

This article gives brief sketches of several older adults who contribute their time and talents to the church. Robert Worley serves as a visitation pastor, Alice Schofer disciples young women, Martha McCombs volunteers as church librarian, and Ed and Nell Beacham organize a craft fair to benefit a local Christian school.

Personal Spiritual Life

MEDITATIONS

Books

398. Anderson, E. (1973). <u>Good morning, Lord: Devotions for the mature years</u>. Grand Rapids, MI: Baker Book House, 95p.

These 54 devotional essays each begin with a line of scripture.

399. Asquith, G. H. (1960). <u>Lively may I walk: Devotions for the golden years</u>. New York: Abingdon, 123p.

This book of 54 meditations is inspirational in tone. The heading or title of each meditation is "The best of. . ." ("The Best of Wisdom," "The Best of Greatness," "The Best of Contentment," etc.).

400. Behnke, C. A. (1959). <u>New frontiers for spiritual living: Devotions for people who are growing spiritually with the years</u>. St. Louis, MO: Concordia, 108p.

Devout and inspirational, this little collection of 55 meditations and selected hymns and prayers seems appropriate for consolation and encouragement.

401. Behnke, C. W. (1965). <u>Today and tomorrow: Devotions for people who are growing with the years</u>. St. Louis, MO: Concordia, 120p.

Forty-seven devotions form this text, inviting the reader to a very positive assessment of life in old age. The mood of the meditations is very upbeat.

402. Bianchi, E. C. (1985). On growing older: A personal guide to life after 35. New York: Crossroad, 148p.

This psycho-spiritual guidebook is written for people who want to age with purpose and grace. The book contains 24 reflections on such critical issues as loneliness, forgiving, loving, suffering, cultivating joy, letting go, peacemaking, and being religious.

403. Brandt, C. (1980). Still time to sing: Prayers & praise for late in life. Minneapolis, MN: Augsburg, 95p.

This book consists of prayers derived from the personal experience of the author who spent several years visiting elderly nursing home patients.

404. Brandt, C. (1977). You're only old once: Devotions in large print. Minneapolis, MN: Augsburg, 126p.

The author is a grandmother who writes to "unlock the secret of a productive life" for older Christians. She addresses topics of special concern, and provides understanding, suggested resources from scripture, and guidance for the reader to see the grace and hope of God.

405. Brandt, L. F. (1984). Bible readings for the retired. Minneaplolis, MN: Augsburg, 110p.

The author uses very brief quotations from 60 Psalms. Each quotation introduces an upbeat and inspirational religious meditation revealing the joys and struggles of the aging psalmists.

406. Buhrig, W. M. (1963). We older people (K. M. S. Easton, Trans.). Valley Forge, PA: Judson, 62p.

Translated from German, this book offers 50 meditations in which the author shares with her contemporaries her experiences as a older person.

407. Champion, J. B. (Ed.). (1983). Reflections of faith: Assemblies of God pioneers sharing memories reflecting on their spiritual heritage. Springfield, MO: Assemblies of God, 79p.

This is a collection of meditations and reflections prepared by older ministers of the Assemblies of God and their families.

408. Doerffler, A. (1945). Treasures of hope. St. Louis, MO: Concordia, 274p.

This large print devotional reader is divided into two sections: the first presents a scripture reading, a prayer, and a hymn for each for four weeks; the second presents prayers for different occasions common to the lives of older Christians (communion, sickness, operations, convalescence, patience, and distress).

409. Dollen, C. (1985). Prayers for a third age. Huntington, IN: Our Sunday Visitor, 185p.

This devotional book for older adults draws upon biblical passages, traditional Catholic prayers, and meditations and writings of saints and others. It is intended to help older adults to look forward to eternal life and prepare for the conclusion of their lives.

410. Eggers, W. T. (1968). Space of joy. St. Louis: MO: Concordia, 222p.

This book of daily morning and evening devotions for four weeks is written to express some of the "sense of wonder and courage and exultation in Christ with .which the Spirit can grace also people who bear the cross of aging bodies. Aware that they yet have much to contribute to a changing world, these older saints still bring warmth to others with the glow of their hearts and lives" (p. 8). The author is an administrator of a Home for Aged Lutherans.

411. Emmons, H. B. (1953). The mature heart. Nashville, TN: Abingdon, 160p.

Writing out of a firmly based Christian faith, the author points to ways of living worthily and serving God and humanity every day. There are 150 meditations in large print for those who seek increasing spiritual strength to enrich the maturing years.

412. Field, L. N. (1970). Rainbows: Reflections for the evening of life. Minneapolis, MN: Augsburg, 134p.

Written for older retired Christians and those approaching retirement, these 38 devotional essays on a variety of everyday subjects grew out of the experiences and observations of the author, a retired pastor and teacher.

413. Finley, J. F. (1989). The treasured age: Spirituality for seniors. New York: Alba House, 114p.

This collection of 50 reflections is divided into six sections: our attitude, the past, prayer, pain/suffering, virtue, seasonal thoughts.

414. Folliet, J. (1983). The evening sun: Growing old beautifully (D. Smith, Trans.). Chicago, IL: Franciscan Herald, 175p.

Translated from French, this charming series of more than 40 brief meditations is so specific to the life and culture of its author that the reader gets a glimpse of the way age and culture are intertwined. This book may serve as a model for writing a journal which reflects finely honed, mature wisdom. It is straightforward, lucid, and inspirational.

415. Gilhuis, C. (1977). Conversations on growing older (C. Barendrecht, Trans.). Grand Rapids, MI: William B. Eerdmans, 175p.

Translated from Dutch, this book of 29 brief meditations is inspirational in tone. The final nine meditations speak of life at the time of death and after death. Much of the book is commonsense encouragement with reference to the Scriptures from a Christian perspective.

416. Hall, E. R. (1978). Looking inward, looking upward. Waco, TX: Word, 205p.

A series of notes from the author's morning meditations in extra large type, this book is inspirational in tone.

417. Keene, M. H. (1976). Patterns for mature living. Nashville, TN: Abingdon, 112p.

This common-sense and inspirational book in large print on everyday life is organized around 48 topics.

418. Kenney, L. F. (1977). Memories and meditations. Philadelphia, PA: Westminster, 154p.

This book of about 75 very brief meditations is a blend of inspiration and common-sense with infrequent references to scripture and religious belief.

419. Lang, P. H. D. (1976). The golden days. St. Louis, MO: Concordia, 111p.

These 30 large print devotions written in traditional devotional format are intended to help older people accept their age and frailties with the knowledge that God will provide them with courage.

420. Lang, P. H. D. (1979). Harvest of faith. St. Louis, MO: Concordia, 96p.

The author, a retired Lutheran minister, has written these reassuring devotionals with photographs of nature scenes in color because "the elderly are above all in need of a right relationship with God through our Savior Jesus Christ" (p. 5).

421. Lauterbach, W. A. (1975). Heaven bound. St. Louis: MO: Concordia, 127p.

This book in sight-saving print is a series of 40 meditations focussed on the journey toward heaven.   The mood of the text is devotional and rather exclusively tied to conservative Christian religious language.

422. Lewis, A. G. (1976). Teach me, Lord: Devotions on basic Christian teachings. Minneapolis, MN: Augsburg, 159p.

It is the intent of the author of these 75 short, positive devotions that they

"...present a summary of basic scriptural teachings in clear, readily legible print" (p. 9) of Christian instruction received in childhood. Among the biblical truths presented are the will of God, creation, redemption, sanctification, prayer, and eternal life.

423. Lockerbie, J. (1982). The quiet moment: Devotions for the golden years. Cincinnati, OH: Standard Publishing, 94p.

It is the hope of the author that the devotions in this book will help older people strengthen their ego, receive hope and purpose, live in the present, make the Bible relevant, and help them realize that God is still present in their lives.

424. Lunde, J. (1967). Light at Eventide (P. Loken, Trans.). Minneapolis, MN: Augsburg, 172p.

This series of 38 brief meditations by Bishop Lunde, known both as "the children's bishop" and the "bishop of the aged," reflects his warmth and devotion.

425. McDonnell, T. P. (1983). Saints in due season: Essays on the art of Christian aging. Huntington, IN: Our Sunday Visitor, 147p.

The author writes about ten saints in their maturity, drawing lessons for today's elderly. Chapters include St. Monica, the persistent mother; St. John Vianney, the well-tempered listener; St. Jerome, the pleasures of irascibility; Job, the problem of suffering; and St. Francis of Assisi, the reconciliation with nature.

426. McEldowney, J. E. (1988). God's presence among the aging: Fifty-five meditations for seniors. Bradenton, FL: The Southmark Foundation on Gerontology, 180p.

These meditations are written to help chaplains and other religious leaders in their work with older people in retirement centers, nursing homes, and hospitals. In addition, "individuals and groups will find in these pages inspiration and insights to help them develop spiritual lifestyles that express faith, hope, and love and relate them to the heart of God" (p. ix).

427. Morgan, R. L. (1990). No wrinkles on the soul. Nashville, TN: Upper

Room Books, 158p.

Morgan, a Presbyterian minister and Older Adult Ministry Enabler, has written 62 meditations for individual or small group devotional use. The meditations are grouped under six themes: life begins every day, tasks of aging, old-age vulnerabilities, no use denying it, keeping the spirit renewed, and ultimate thoughts.

428. Morrison, R., & Radtke, D. D. (1988). Aging with joy. Mystic, CT: Twenty-third, 103p.

This book offers practical guidelines, in 17 brief chapters, so that aging will not be simply endured but will be lived with joy. The authors are psychotherapists, and some of their strategies reflect expertise in communication of feelings with others and self.

429. Murphey, C. (1988). Day to day: Spiritual help when someone you love has Alzheimer's. Philadelphia, PA: Westminster, 152p.

This daily devotional and prayer guide for friends and family supporting a loved one diagnosed with Alzheimer's disease is organized into chapters based on the stages of the disease.

430. Nixon, J. L. (1979). The grandmother's book. Nashville, TN: Abingdon, 63p.

A little book of reflections about the everyday--but no less marvelous for that--events of being a new grandmother. Each of 19 very brief reflections ends with a verse from scripture.

431. Nystedt, O. (1956). Fast falls the eventide: Words for devotion and contemplation (C. A. Nelson, Trans.). Rock Island, IL: Augustana, 96p.

Translated from Swedish, this is a book of short, traditional devotional readings beginning with a line of scripture and ending with a poem or hymn.

432. O'Flaherty, V. M. (1976). The grace of old age: An essay. Chicago, IL: Franciscan Herald, 64p.

This little book consisting of one essay is divided into 64 sections which can be used for daily meditation. The essay is the result of the author's thoughts about the purpose of old age.

433. Patterson, L. (1986). The best is yet to be: 85 inspirational devotions for the retirement years. Wheaton, IL: Tyndale House, 220p.

Eighty-five short devotionals on topics of interest to adults approaching retirement are written by a former chaplain of Wheaton College.

434. Reynolds, L. R. (1984). No retirement: Devotions on Christian discipleship for older people. Philadelphia, PA: Fortress, 95p.

Written from a positive but realistic perspective on later years, the author offers contemporary and practical devotions for older persons with increased freedom. Scripture reading and a line from well-known hymns begin each devotional.

435. Robertson, J. (1974). Meditations for the later years. Nashville, TN: Abingdon, 80p.

These brief, large print devotions use quotes from well-known sources to begin inspirational messages and prayers to end them.

436. Robertson, J. (1965). Saying yes to life: As we grow older. Nashville, TN: Abingdon, 144p.

This book of 44 brief meditations tells human interest stories of the lives of men and women who deal with common problems in a positive way. The key to contentment is to say "yes" to what one is and can do, and to do this with one's whole heart.

437. Rommel, K. (1975). The best is yet to be (D. Scheidt, Trans.). Philadelphia, PA: Fortress, 77p.

Translated from German, these 25 reflections are simple, practical statements that go to the heart of an older person's life and relationships. Photographs complement and reaffirm the text.

438. Rudd, E. (1976). God makes old age young (J. M. Moe, Trans.).
Minneapolis, MN: Augsburg, 176p.

Translated from Norwegian, this book of 39 brief meditations in large print is
inspirational in tone and religious in focus. The book speaks to the needs,
questions, and feelings of older people with words of comfort and challenge
taken from the Scriptures and from the author's understanding of Christian
faith.

439. Swanson, D. V. (1966). Life's crowning years: A book of inspiration.
Philadelphia, PA: Fortress, 122p.

Forty brief meditations form this devotional text.   The author, a retired
minister, has avoided a problem-centered approach and has written inspirational
meditations with explicitly religious and biblical references on a variety of
topics.

440. Swift, H. C. (1986). Prayers for sunset years: Eleven
simple ways to spend time with God.   Cincinnati, OH: St. Anthony
Messenger, 53p.

In each of the book's 11 sections the author deals with themes especially
pertinent to older adult Christians, offering concrete suggestions and specific
steps that enable the reader to creatively move closer to God.

441. Syverson, B. G. (1987). Bible readings for caregivers. Minneapolis,
MN: Augsburg, 108p.

A collection of one-page devotional readings based on scripture verses applied
to medical experiences of the author (a nurse) and other contributors.

442. Wisloff, H. E. (1969). Safe in his arms (J. M. Njus, Trans.).
Minneapolis, MN: Augsburg, 94p.

In this collection of 30 brief meditations the author deals with some of the
problems that elderly people have said they think about and struggle with:
loneliness, doubts, sorrow, temptations, death, eternal life, Christian witness,
the dark night of the spirit.

THE DEVOUT LIFE: AUTHOR IDENTIFIED AS A SENIOR

Books

443. Alexander, A. (1844).   Letters to the aged. In Thoughts on religious experience. Philadelphia, PA: Presbyterian Board of Publication.

The author writes five letters as an aged man concerning the need to not sink into despondency as we consider past failures, the endeavor to be useful, the peculiar duties incumbent on the aged, the solemn event of our departure from this life, and rendering death safe and comfortable. The author's thought is informed by acute personal reflection and observation, a wide Christian vision, and a vigorous faith.

444. Barnes, A. (1858).   Life at three-score. Philadelphia, PA: Parry & McMillan, 78p.

This sermon was delivered in the First Presbyterian Church, Philadelphia, November 28, 1856. The author, three days before his sixtieth birthday, feels that someone his age ought to be able to say something "bright and hopeful in regard to the prospects which are to open upon the world which he is soon to leave--bright and hopeful in regard to the world to which he is so soon to go" (p. 10). He finds great value in life itself, that life is willing to aid the young; he praises temperance, industry, and religion; he is at life's end, hopeful.

445. Coupland, S. (1985).   Beginning to pray in old age. Cambridge, MA: Cowley, 80p.

This book, well grounded in Christian tradition, addresses the special concern of parishioners who seek to begin or renew their lives of prayer later in life. The author makes suggestions on helpful reading and making private retreats, offers examples of appropriate short prayers, and gives advice on ways to cope with the physical limitations of aging when they arise along the spiritual journey.

446. Custer, C. E. (Ed.). (1986).   The gift of maturity. Nashville, TN: Discipleship Resources, 37p.

In this small book, seven older adult authors share their images of the aging process from their vantage point in brief, inspirational essays: Aging as a spiritual journey, the gains and losses of aging, caring for one another, facing death, sources of strength, leaving a heritage, and called to servanthood.

447. Fisher, E. (1987). Good ways of growing older. Mahwah, NJ: Paulist, 230p.

A former journalist, historian, filmmaker and professor of American Studies at the University of Notre Dame writes his reflection on growing older.

448. Knox, J. (1985). A glory in it all: Reflections after eighty. Waco, TX: Word, 150p.

A book of reflective essays on a variety of subjects written in the author's ninth decade. A few topics are possession, greatness, God's strange gift, education and the human spirit, forgiving oneself, and taking death in stride.

449. LaFarge, J. (1963). Reflections on growing old. Chicago, IL: Loyola University, 137p.

This book begins with the assumption that "old age has its own meaning, like other phases of human life, and that the wisest thing to do, when old age has crept up on us, would be to explore that meaning and to adopt some general plan of action, so as really to profit by it" (p. 11). The author, a well-known Jesuit priest and journalist in his mid-eighties, presents his view of old age in five chapters: "Growth-Through-Diminishment," "Our Steadfast Hope," "The Power of Love," "Society's Responsibility," and "Courage in Old Age".

450. Robinson, G. L. (1951). Live out your years. New York: Abelard, 114p.

Written by a retired seminary professor in his mid-eighties, this little book is a collection of literary pieces woven together with the author's reflections. His preface is worth quoting in toto: "This brief postscript, so to speak, to my literary life is intended especially for those who realize the march of time and the reckoning of the years; for those, also, who long for comfort, and wish to face the end without fear; in particular, for those to whom the days seem shorter and the nights longer".

451. Taylor, F. M. (1979). You don't have to be old when you grow old. Plainfield, NJ: Logos International, 116p.

In this book a great-grandmother expresses deep faith in God and in rich personal family relationships. Chapters include "Old Age: Its Difficulties;" "Old Age: Its Challenges and Opportunities;" "Three Generation Homes;" "A Faith for Old Age".

Articles

452. Olitzky, K. M. (Ed.). (1990, Spring). Reflections on growing older: A Journal of Aging and Judaism Symposium. The Journal of Aging and Judaism, 4, 185-219.

A dozen older members of the Jewish community, leaders for generations, reflect on their own aging. They provide insights from real life in their musings and philosophical contemplation. These brief essays might serve as a basis for discussion or for personal and group reflection.

453. Sittler, J. (1987, Winter). The last lecture: A walk around truth, eternal life, faith. Religion and Intellectual Life, 4, 59-65.

The author reflects on three things which, he notes, have been on his mind "since I had a mind that was aware of the world at all: the nature of truth; what the scripture means by eternal life; and the nature of faith" (p. 59). This essay is the author's testimony about his enduring beliefs, which include a conviction that the Christian story is most adequate to describe what he knows about human life. He also affirms that the "scattered life, which does not admire and is thus not drawn toward anything better than episodic sensation, which has no center, no value toward which it is drawn, is self-destructive" (p. 65).

THE DEVOUT LIFE: AUTHOR NOT IDENTIFIED AS A SENIOR

Books

454. Bentley, V. (1975). The beauty of age. Dallas, TX: Temple, 96p.

Five of the chapters of this book were originally sermons, two are condensations of class material. The tone of this little book is inspirational; the Bible is used to support the author's insights on the beauty of age.

455. Deeken, A. (1972). <u>Growing old, and how to cope with it</u>. New York: Paulist, 103p.

This slight devotional text is a thoughtful and literary reflection on age from a parish priest. It has many practical suggestions for working out the problems of age, for building up self-respect, for dealing with worries, pain, unexpected events, loneliness. Most striking features of the text are its numerous references to a wide range of literature and its level of insight.

456. Haschek, P. (1979). <u>Evening with God: Thoughts and prayers</u> (D. Smith, Trans.). Chicago, IL: Franciscan Herald, 233p.

This translation from the Dutch edition of a German work encourages the practice of prayer and offers aids for prayer in old age. Prayers and thoughtful quotations (with accompanying scripture readings) are organized in seven sections. The prayers and quotations range from Shaw, Tolstoi, de Beauvoir, Huxley, Bernanos and Kierkegaard to a wide selection from the Classics of Western Spirituality.

457. Maitland, D. J. (1987). <u>Aging: A time for new learning</u>. Atlanta, GA: John Knox, 133p.

The author views aging as a time for coming to terms with God, realizing life's potential, discovering the experience of years, and reflecting on the fulfillment of life.

458. Maurus, J. (1976). <u>Growing old gracefully</u>. Canfield, OH: Alba Books, 117p.

A common-sense and inspirational little book, this is fairly characteristic of that genre of literature of the 1970s.

459. Mooney, P. J. (1983). <u>A gift of love: Remembering the old anew</u>. Mystic, CT: Twenty-Third Publications, 47p.

This pocket size poetic, inspirational book is dedicated to the author's father. Black and white photographs taken throughout his father's life are interspersed with verse affirming his long life.

460. Narramore, C. M. (1961). The mature years. Grand Rapids, MI: Zondervan, 58p.

This little book is in the Christian Psychology Series published by Zondervan Publications. Inspirational and common-sensical, it concludes with a poem, "I Am Not Old".

461. Orton, J. (1980). Discourses to the aged. New York: New York Times, 340p.

This volume is a reprint from the best available copy of the 1801 edition printed by J. Cushing, Salem. It contains sermons, delivered on "the last Lord's days of successive years; it being my custom, on those days, to address more immediately to my aged friends" (p. v). Topics include the fruitfulness of aged Christians; the design and improvement of useless days and wearisome nights; God's promise to bear and deliver his aged servants; the outward man decaying, and the inward man renewing; the honor of aged piety; the joy of the aged in leaving their descendants prosperous, peaceful and pious; and the hand of God in removing our friends far from us.

462. Wisloff, F. (1967). The evening of life (A. Unhjem, Trans.). Philadelphia, PA: Fortress, 132p.

Translated from Norwegian, this inspirational book, reflecting as it does another culture, has enough differences to spark modest interest in what is otherwise a fairly positive but stereotypical devotional text about old age.

Articles

463. Browne, C. E. (1988, April). The best is yet to be. Fundamentalist Journal, 7, 36-38.

Old age can be viewed as a time of physical and mental decline, or from the more hopeful Christian perspective--a time of progressing from the immaturity of childhood to physical, mental, and spiritual maturity. The later can only be fulfilled when we see Christ. Our attitudes and lifestyle will determine what kind of older person we will be.

464. Fisher, E. (1978, March). Aging as worship. Worship, 52, 98-108.

Old age is a vocation which brings an inner balance that improves with the years. Virtues of old age include patience, giving courage to those on the way, discipline, freedom from self-pity and bitterness, serenity and wholeness, and having the courage of one's doubts. Old age shows the narrowness of any religious view but may also bring great delight. The old need to find an abiding interest brings satisfaction and allows them to pursue the inner life.

465. Grudem, W. (1986). Aging inside-out. Christianity Today, 30, 32.

The Christian understanding of aging is based on a paradox: with the increase in years comes spiritual growth.

466. Kelley, W. V. (1906, January). Life's seasons. Methodist Review, 88, 113-116.

This editorial reflects on a human tendency to shrink from life's later seasons. In a tone reminiscent of Victorian morality the author states, "It has been well said that all lines of the human face have something either touching or grand, unless they seem to come from low passions or evil habits" (p. 115).

SPIRITUAL DEVELOPMENT AND GROWTH

Books

467a. Chinen, A. B. (1989). In the ever after: Fairy tales and the second half of life. Wilmette, IL: Chiron, 203p.

The author has gathered together 15 fairy tales in which the protagonists are older adults. On their own terms these delightful stories are full of intuitive wisdom about late life. Chinen draws out from these fairy tales a psychology and spirituality of maturity, revealing the developmental tasks of the second half of life. His psychoanalytic and Jungian perspectives yield a rich interpretation of old age.

467b. Ford, I. M. (1988). Life spirals: The faith journey. Burlington, Ontario: Welch, 100p.

The author presents her model of faith development and illustrates it with her own faith journey.

468. Marty, M. E. (1983). A cry of absence: Reflections for the winter of the heart. San Francisco, CA: Harper & Row, 172p.

While this book is not addressed specifically to the topic of aging, it examines a metaphor which may be of particular help in a period of life in which the probability of losses increases. It traces a spiritual journey that has been described as the dark night of the soul, the cloud of unknowing, the negative way to God, and shows the possibility of insight, strength, endurance, and a sure, sober faith.

469. Peckham, C. W., & Peckham, A. B. (1979). I can still pray: A guidebook for ministers, lay persons, families and students who are interested in the spiritual needs of the elderly. Lebanon, OH: Otterbein Home, 230p.

While the authors of this book have tried to write from an interfaith perspective, they admit that there is a Christian bias. Part I discusses spiritual needs of the aging person. Part II is a collection of essays writen by the residents and staff of the Otterbein Home on the experienced or observed spiritual changes of older people. Part III summarizes a study conducted with 349 older persons in southwest Ohio on their faith commitment. In this small sample, faith commitment tended to increase with age. Part IV focuses on the development of aging ministries.

470. Simmons, H. C. (1992). In the footsteps of the mystics: A beginner's guide to the spiritual classics. New York: Paulist.

This book is designed to bring older adults and others into conversation with the mystics--those women and men whose writings are known collectively as the Classics of Western Spirituality. It is organized around a series of questions about the spiritual life: about prayer, the presence of God, failure and grace, the community of faith, and love. The selections from the mystics (Muslim, Jewish, Christian, and Native American, spanning 15 centuries) respect individual approaches to prayer, invite personal reflection, and help readers value their own life answers. The book was developed in conversation with seniors and others in churches, retirement homes, congregate meal sites, and retreat settings.

471. Van Kaam, A. (1979). The transcendent self: The formative spirituality of middle, early and later years of life. Denville, NJ: Dimension Books, 202p.

While the focus of this book (despite the subtitle) is the transcendent self and the mid-life crisis, the author's careful attention to this reality does have implications for detachment in the second half of life. As well, older adults who have not dealt well with the mid-life crisis may have to renegotiate aspects of this crucial time of self-transcendence.

Articles

472. Ammerman, C. (1990). Spiritual dimension of human sexuality. Journal of Religious Gerontology, 7(1/2), 83-98.

This essay considers its topic with a variety of approaches, noting the inevitability of loss, the need for a poetic language, the relationship between sexuality and spiritual pilgrimage in religious writings, and acquiescence.

473. Borelli, J. (1982). The paradigm of aging. In F. V. Tiso (Ed.), Aging: Spiritual perspectives (pp. 185-193). Lake Worth, FL: Sunday Publications.

A study of aging from a Jungian perspective, including images of wise old man and earth mother, affirms the profoundly spiritual quality of life. The self passes from a mere collection of self-images to confrontation with a truth and reality greater than the individual, namely the image of God within each person.

474. Brownlee, A. G. (1984, Winter). The dark night of hope. Journal of Religion & Aging, 1(2), 9-25.

Using the writings of Gabriel Marcel as a starting point, this essay argues that hope occurs between persons--it is not an isolated, private act. This discussion may be of help when working with older people who say they have nothing left for which to hope.

475. Clements, W. M. (1985-1986, Fall/Winter). Aging and the dimensions of spiritual development. Journal of Religion & Aging, 2(1/2), 127-36.

The spiritual development of older persons requires attention to the roles of memory and critical anticipation in spiritual development: memory as the past's continuation and source of identity, and critical anticipation as a vision of the future. The spiritual development of the elderly may be hampered by a youth-oriented view of time that denies the anticipation necessary for spiritual creativity.   The article presents two strategies for spiritual development: religious biography and a database called religious gerontology.

476. Clements, W. M. (1979). The sense of life time in human development. Journal of Religion and Health, 18, 88-92.

Issues of identity and growth take place in the medium of the subjective sense of life time. This article examines life time in middle age (which focusses on time remaining), in early old age (in which attention tends to focus on past time), and in old age (in which the experience of "now" frees the person from the bondage of time as perceived earlier. The old adult must learn to find direction and creativity without a distant future for orientation.

477. Clements, W. M. (1990). Spiritual development in the fourth quarter of life. Journal of Religious Gerontology, 7(1/2), 55-70.

This article discusses ages 75 to 100. In that period a dominant sense of time facilitates spiritual development, which is the dominant task of the fourth quarter of life.   Meaning making--the desire and ability to make sense of existence and to draw together an understanding of the path of one's life--is best done in the fourth quarter of life.

478. Gillman, N.   (1985/1986, Winter).   Judaism and the search for spirituality. Conservative Judaism, 38(2), 518.

While assiduously avoiding any definition of spirituality that would devalue the human body or promote any other-worldly eschatology, the author examines three models of spirituality: 1) the behavioral (what God wants above all is for the community to walk in His ways, to observe His commandments), 2) the pietistic (what God wants above all is inner devotion), and 3) the intellectual (what God wants above all is knowledge, understanding, the mind). Each is rooted in classical formulation of Judaism, although emerging at different eras.

"Each implies a curriculum for the education of the believer. Each determines what should take place within the synagogue, the home, the academy or on the street" (p. 6). (See citation no. 498).

479. Gratton, C. (1980, November). Summaries of books relevant to the topic of spirituality and aging. Studies in Formative Spirituality, 1, 481-95.

Gratton reviews six books that address the experience of aging and ways in which the inner self transcends material considerations. A selected bibliography follows; it considers supplementary texts that broadly incorporate issues of aging from philosophical, theological and mystical-ascetical points of view to set directions and from the social sciences and humanities to ground a study of aging.

480. Guinan, Sr. St. Michael. (1971). Maturation and aging. Maturity and Religious Life, Donum Dei, Monograph of the Canadian Religious Conference, 15, 83-103.

This philosophical and psychological study contrasts the Outer Man of late 20th century with the Inner Man. Ages and stages of Metaphysical Man are developed in a Christian context.

481. Hall, E. G. (1985, Winter). Spirituality during aging. Pastoral Psychology, 34, 112-117.

Allport's description of mature religious sentiment and Jung's perspective on the psychodynamics of the human spirit are compared. This forms the basis for examining three case studies of old adults who typify different aspects of mature spirituality: self-worth drawn from the role of spiritual elder rather than from role of family care-taker, the develoment of a way to value personal life which is not dependent on physical well-being, and identification with the transcendent nature of the human spirit so as to transcend physical limitations. Attention to spirituality may augment a simply developmental approach to age.

482. Jones, W. P. (1984, Fall). Aging as a spiritualizing process. Journal of Religion & Aging, 1(1), 3-16.

This article identifies 11 dimensions of the aging process that may lead to a new spirituality rather than increased religiousity. These dimensions are anamnesis, sacramentalizing, enfleshment, contingency, reversal, doing-being, confidant at paradigm, the whimsical, the dialogical, epiclesis, and resignation of trust.

483. Kohlberg, L. (1973, Winter). Stages and aging in moral development: Some speculations. The Gerontologist, 13, 497-502.

This article reviews Kohlberg's theory of moral development and discusses aspects of adult moral development both in Stages 5 and 6, and in an hypothesized Stage 7 which is unique to advanced adulthood and involves adoption of a religious and cosmic perspective.

484. Kollar, N. R. (1985, Spring). Towards a spirituality of aging and old age. Journal of Religion & Aging, 1(3), 49-59.

"This article demonstrates that process of aging is itself a religious activity. It claims that if in our later years, aging is done in an authentically human way, it leads to the growth and improvement of society" (p. 50). Three aspects of the aging process reveal three rhythms of religious life: transition from one stage to the next (conversion); losses and gains (death-resurrection); and the realization that there is more to life than the present (transcendence). There are also the tensions of the finite and infinite, mortality and immortality.

485. McFadden, S. H. (1985, Spring). Attributes of religious maturity in aging people. Journal of Religion & Aging, 1(3), 39-48.

This essay looks at religious maturity viewed from the way older people remember their past, experience their present, and anticipate their future. Erikson's idea of ego integrity provides a model for describing these characteristics of religious maturity.

486. Mills, R. (1990, Winter). To life! Spirituality and health care in the aging years. The Journal of Aging and Judaism, 5, 95-145.

Eleven papers are included from a symposium held at Temple Shalom, Chicago. Essays range from David Gutmann's "Strength or Stigma: The Aging Stranger," to Lucille H. Davis, "The Black Church and African-American Elders," and Perry LeFevre's "Religious Organizations; Response to Needs." Linda Vogel's "Establishing Spiritual Community in Residential and Long-Term Care Settings" appears in the next issue, Vol. 5, No. 3, as do papers by Sanford and Rhoma Finkel, "Judiasm and Mental

Health in the Later Years," and Finny Casey et al., "Selected Nursing Interventions for Spiritual Needs of the Elderly in Acute Care Settings".

487. Missinne, L. E. (1990). Christian perspectives on spiritual needs of a human being. Journal of Religious Gerontology, 7(1/2), 143-152.

Spiritual needs, integral to human life are not separated from biological, social, psychological, and material aspects of life. Some specific tasks of older people, based on contemporary Christian spirituality, are commitment to justice, peace, the environment, and a deeper bond of love for God and neighbor.

488. Payne, B. (1990). Spiritual maturity and meaning-filled relationships: A sociological perspective. Journal of Religious Gerontology, 7(1/2), 25-40.

This article applies Atchley's four stages in the process of retirement to the case of Sarah-Patton Boyle in order to describe the process of self-development, spiritual maturity, and the construction of new and meaningful relationships in late life. Boyle's case identifies changes in her social roles and relationships and her struggle to keep a positive view of herself in the midst of socio-environmental changes. Also discussed are her struggle for identity as a spiritual self and ties with the church.

489. Poling, J. (1989). Old age: A time of crisis. Journal of Religion & Aging, 5(4), 31-41.

Ageism, sexism, and racism, combined with the crises of loss, physical decline, and social oppression make old age a spiritually difficult time for many older persons. The author recommends the development of images for the latter part of life that are honest with both dangers and possibilities. Old age is open without limit to spiritual growth and depth in relationship with God.

490. Shulik, R. (1988). Faith development in older adults. Educational Gerontology, 14, 291-301.

This paper introduces the faith development paradigm of James Fowler and reviews a research project in which that paradigm was applied to older adults.

491. Simmons, H. C. (1976, March/April). The quiet journey: Psychological

development and religious growth from ages thirty to sixty.   Religious Education, 71, 132-142.

This article shows the possibility of real inner process and development common to adults during the years from 30 to 60.   These issues are of importance for older adults to the extent that they remain as unfulfilled or incomplete tasks--unrecognized, unshared, or unsupported by a community of faith.

492. Snyder, R. (1981, September/October). Religious meaning and the latter third of life. Religious Education, 76, 534-52.

Snyder explores elements of meaning in the latter third of life.   Areas of meaning formation are the saga of one's life and memberships (congregations and peer culture).   He suggests that an ethical life is a structure, and in the latter third of life people might take responsibility for formation of structures which hold civilization together while providing a sense of purpose for their lives.   Snyder contends that the human spirit is a system of meanings. Meaning is developmental, collaborative, and integral to life; it focuses on reality.   Religious meaning promises the continuity of transgenerational existence.

493. Soucie, L. (1987, Fall). Has aging a meaning? Anima, 14(1), 65-68.

In this essay, sculpting becomes a metaphor for finding the meaning in aging. As in sculpting, the meaning is "contained within the aging process itself, as within a stone or piece of clay" (p. 68).

494. Stokes, K. (1990). Faith development in the adult life cycle. Journal of Religious Gerontology, 7(1/2), 167-184.

The Faith Development in the Adult Life Cycle Project found that faith development is not significantly related to age, that men's and women's approaches to faith development are subtly different, and that psycho-social health and faith development are positively correlated.

495. Strunk, O. (1984, Winter). The therapeutic use of devotional reading in working with the aging. Journal of Religion & Aging, 1, 1-8.

This article presents three principles to help older adults benefit from reading devotional literature used as an adjunct to psychotherapy--a specific genre of bibliotherapy. General principles to guide the therapist in this activity are 1) become familiar with the literature, 2) assess the possible symbiotic relation between readings and lifestyle of older person, and 3) maintain a continuing caring relationship with the person involved in a devotional reading program.

496. Teasdale, W. (1982). The mystical dimension of aging. In F. V. Tiso (Ed.), Aging: Spiritual perspectives (pp. 221-248). Lake Worth, FL: Sunday Publications.

The mystical life, as understood in all the religions of the world, goes through three stages or levels of spiritual growth in the process of contemplative aging. These stages include purgation (detachment from self-will and egocentricity), illumination (with the perception of God's presence in all things and the relationship of all things to God), and union (the permanent perception of mystical experience). The author joins this understanding to that of contemplation and the transformation of the earth.

497. Waxman, B. F. (1985, Fall). From Bildungsroman to Reifungsroman: Aging in Doris Lessing's Fiction. Soundings: An Interdisciplinary Journal, 68, 318-334.

This article explores personal and spiritual maturity for women in middle and old age in two novels by Doris Lessing, The Summer Before the Dark, and The Diary of a Good Neighbor. Old age for a woman, according to Lessing, is far from being a dark period of a woman's life. Old age may offer the opportunity for "sun-drenched" spiritual growth and increasing self-appreciation. Lessing tells her readers to look forward to the shedding of their sexuality as liberation and empowerment. Lessing's optimistic message is that the "bridge between middle age and old age is one that can liberate a woman from an inhibiting fear of death and enable her to develop true self-respect, to become more receptive to relationships with others" (p. 321).

498. Weisman, C. B., & Schwartz, P. (1989, Spring). Spirituality: An integral part of aging. The Journal of Aging and Judaism, 3, 110-115.

This article defines spirituality as the concept of self. Following Neil Gillman (see citation no. 478), three models are identified: behavioral (patterns of behavior are based on response to covenant through obedience to the law), pietistic (union with God is manifested through emotional expression), and intellectual (study of the Book, the primary means to discover God's will). Spirituality nourishes identity, develops wisdom, and creates opportunity for creativity and inner growth.

Dissertations

499. Dillon, D. L. (1988). Enabling the laity to grow spiritually and to fulfill their ministries through the local church: Group spiritual direction and adult faith development (Doctor of Ministry thesis, Drew University). DAI, 49, 1829A.

This project studied spiritual direction in a group setting, integrating insights from Erik Erikson, Carl Jung, and James Fowler with a theological interpretation of Christian spiritual direction. It indicates that evangelism and small group interaction for spiritual growth complement each other in local church vitalization.

500. McFadden, S. H. (1984). The wisdom and humor of aging persons: Perspectives on transformed narcissism in later life (Doctor of Philosophy dissertation, Drew University). DAI, 46, 1714B.

The psychological dimension of wisdom and humor require a paradoxical perspective on the self and the world (here referred to as "involved detachment"). The author asks why some aging persons readily achieve these transformations of narcissism while others do not. The position is taken that the fundamental issues of aging can be interpreted as religious. Wisdom and humor of aging persons who have appropriate ego integrity function as expressions of faith.   Those who have acheived a sense of ego integrity, wisdom and humor communicate what Erik Erikson calls generative love.

501. Parry, B. J. (1984/1986). Wisdom: Investigation of a construct (Doctor of Philosophy thesis, California School of Professional Psychology, Fresno). DAI, 47, 385B.

This study hypothesized wisdom as a composite construct composed of seven predicted variables.   Three age groups were tested to inquire about differentiation. Results indicated no support for the principal hypothesis; age groups were differentiated on individual variables.

502. Putt, R. A. (1988). The design of a method for helping middle age adults in faith development (Doctor of Ministry thesis, Drew University). DAI, 49, 3390A.

This project used a group setting, with discussion and feedback, to help those in middle adulthood to view individual concerns and issues in the light of faith. The proposed design helped in a process of liberation of the mid-life adult caught between young adult children and aging or dying parents.

SPIRITUAL WELL-BEING

Books

503. Cook, T. C. (1981, February). An age integrated society: Implications for spiritual well-being. Washington, DC: White House Conference on Aging, 65p.

This report is comprised of eight sections: introduction, conceptual framework, data base, present situation, trends to 1980 and beyond, major findings, key issues and recommendations. Spiritual well-being is identified as a bridging term in a sociological as well as religious sense. It "is essential that there be some common denominator or catch word to allude to qualities of being human which, if overlooked or undermined, seriously damages personhood and self worth" (p. 5).

504. Cook, T. C. (1976). The religious sector explores its mission in aging: A report on the survey of programs for the aging under religious auspices. Athens, GA: National Interfaith Coalition on Aging, 164p.

This project report is in three parts: research information in the religious sector; data; and education. It contains an annotated bibliography and an appendix which responds to the spiritual well-being recommendations of the 1971 White House Conference on Aging.

505. Cook, T. C. (Ed.). (1983, Fall). Religion and aging. Generations, 8(1).

This issue offers brief reflections on religion and aging on a variety of topics: denominational mission, spiritual well-being, program planning, interfaith cooperation, interaction between the church and the aging network, church based advocacy, and model projects. The article by Linda-Marie Delloff on the exclusion of religionists from the 1981 White House Conference on Aging gives a specific historical account of an important shift in the relationship between the religious sector and the government.

506a. Moberg, D. O. (Ed.).   (1979).   Spiritual well-being: Sociological perspectives. Washington, DC: University Press.

This remarkable collection of essays includes an introduction and conclusion by David Moberg, and 22 other essays in 4 categories: 1) conceptual studies of spiritual well-being, 2) spiritual well-being and sociological theory, 3) qualitative research on SWB, and 4) quantitative research on SWB. The quality, specificity, and scope of the essays are of a high standard.

506b. Thorson, J. A., & Cook, T. C. (Eds.). (1980). Spiritual well-being of the elderly. Springfield, IL: Charles C. Thomas, 238p.

The 30 chapters of this book discuss spiritual well-being itself in relation to God, self, the community, and the environment. This book sought to map out the common ground between gerontology, theology, and philosophy. Authors represent the disciplines of sociology, adult education, psychology, social work, philosophy, anthropology, counseling, and nursing. In theology, authors write from Jewish (Orthodox) and Christian (Protestant, Catholic) perspectives. The book was a culmination of a period of intense exploration of religion and aging under the rubric of spiritual well-being.

507. White House Conference on Aging, 1971. (1971).   Section recommendations on Spiritual Well-Being.   Washington, DC: U.S. Government Printing Office, 10p.

Fourteen recommendations are developed by 198 participants of the Spiritual Well-Being Section, chaired by Arthur S. Flemming. This foundational document for the study of spiritual well-being as a public concept structures the relationship between the religious community, the government, and the aging.

Articles

508. Barden, A. K. (1985-1986, Fall/Winter).   Toward new directions for ministry in aging: An overview of issues and concepts. Journal of Religion

& Aging, 2(1/2), 137-50.

The author questions the adequacy of psychosocial aging theories in providing for older persons' spiritual well-being. Barden discusses religion, religiosity, theology, spirituality, and ministry, and explores their function in the conceptual development of spiritual aging. He finds that Shalom guides an assessment of spiritual well-being: "the fullness of life which is the state of living in harmony with all humanity, having financial prosperity, good health, peace of mind, and the free growth of the inner soul" (p. 145).

509. Becker, A. H. (1986, Spring). Pastoral theological implications of the aging process. Journal of Religion & Aging, 2(3), 13-30.

Major spiritual-theological issues for the aging are clarified by attention to three epochs of aging. The young-old ask, "What shall I do with my life?" the middle old ask, "What about my dying?" and the old-old ask, "Why must I suffer so?" Pastoral ministry addresses each of these faith concerns by using the life review as a reflective tool to examine God's providence throughout the older person's life.

510. Becker, A. H. (1980, Winter). Values and aging. Theological Education, 16, 341-345.

Becker writes that caring relationships are central to spiritual well-being and part of a matrix that includes one's relationship to God, family, friends and the larger community. The author discusses interrelated autonomy, personal respect, contributions, change/growth, and hope. These values are an important motivational core for seminary teaching.

511. Birren, J. E. (1990). Spiritual maturity in psychological development. Journal of Religious Gerontology, 7(1/2), 41-54.

The author discusses a change in orientation in the latter part of life from a logical analytical orientation to an interior affective focus. A review of data from 13 countries indicates an increase with age of the acceptance of the conditions of life, and the role of age, gender, and cultural differences in religious belief.

512. Delloff, L. M. (1981, December 16). Democracy in action and inaction.

The Christian Century, 98, 1299-1300.

See below "Mr. Barclay goes to Washington: Religion at the White House Conference on Aging".

513. Delloff, L. M. (1981, December 30). Mr. Barclay goes to Washington: Religion at the White House Conference on Aging. The Christian Century, 98, 1363-1366.

Despite lengthy and rigorous preparation, in particular (but not exclusively) through the National Interfaith Coalition on Aging, the religious community perceived itself purposely and systematically excluded from the White House Conference. The response of the religious sector was that it would, in spite of the administration, get involved. The story is told with passion and precise detail. An earlier editorial by the same author, "Democracy in action and inaction," helps set the scene for what occurred. Together, these articles are an important record of the involvement of the religious community in the 1981 White House Conference on Aging.

514. Delloff, L. M. (1979, May 2). "Rise up before the hoary head". The Christian Centruy, 96, 483-85.

Editorial comment on the 1979 meeting of the National Interfaith Coalition on Aging, this article is a record of goals, strategies, and implementation of projects.

515. Ellison, C. G., Gay, D. A., & Glass, T. A. (1989, September). Does religious commitment contribute to individual life satisfaction? Social Forces, 68(1), 100-123.

Although this article does not use age as a variable, it is of interest for the questions it raises and for possible connections and overlaps with the term "spiritual well-being." The article specifies the relationships between three dimensions of religiosity (affiliation, participation, and devotion) and one particular facet of well-being, namely general life satisfaction. Devotional (private) and participatory (public) aspects of religiosity have relatively small but persistent positive relationships with life satisfaction.   Certain denominational affiliations (Southern Baptist and "Other Baptist") are positively associated with satisfaction beyond the mere effect of higher levels of social participation.

516. Ellison, C. G., & Gay, D. A. (1990). Region, religious commitment, and life satisfaction among Black Americans. The Sociological Quarterly, 31(1), 123-147.

Using data from the National Survey of Black Americans, the authors study determinants of life satisfaction for Blacks. The study shows that religious participation and subjective well-being are correlated only among non-southern Blacks and that private religiosity is unrelated to well-being. Denominational effects are also noted: non-southern members of traditional Black denominations (e.g., Baptists and Methodists) and southern Catholics report particularly high levels of life satisfaction.

517. Ellison, C. W. (1983). Spiritual well-being: Conceptualization and measurement. Journal of Psychology and Theology, 11, 330-340.

This article reports the development of a scale to measure spiritual well-being. All items deal with transcendent concerns--those aspects of experience which involve relationship to God, faith, commitment, purpose in life, meaning, and ideals. The article discusses the conceptualization of the scale and offers suggestions for further research.

518. Hateley, B. J. (1984, Winter). Spiritual well-being through life histories. Journal of Religion & Aging, 1(2), 63-71.

Hateley outlines an adult education program for churches entitled "Telling Your Story, Exploring Your Faith: Autobiography for Personal Insight and Spiritual Growth." She explains that this course is one way to demonstrate the close connection between psychological well-being and spiritual well-being. The course uses three educational strategies: lectures, writing assignments, and small group discussions. While designed for Protestant Christian groups, suggestions are included for adapting the program to other settings.

519. Koenig, H. G., Kvale, J. N., & Ferrel, C. (1988). Religion and well-being in later life. The Gerontologist, 28, 18-28.

A study of 836 older adults showed moderately strong correlation between morale and three measures: organized religious activity, non-organized religious activity, and intrinsic religiosity. For women and those over 75 religious behaviors and attitudes were particularly strong correlates of morale. The relationship between morale and religion may indicate a need for an expanded role for religious professionals in the delivery of mental health services.

520. Levin, J. S., & Markides, K. (1988). Religious attendance and psychological well-being in middle-aged and older Mexican Americans. Sociological Analysis, 49(1), 66-72.

In "the case of religious attendance as a determinant of psychological well-being, and even of morbidity and mortality, there is a growing concensus supported by data [...] suggesting that religious attendance fails to capture a meaningful 'religious' effect and, instead, may be largely a proxy for health status, especially among older subjects" (p. 70).

521. Moberg, D. O. (1990). Spiritual maturity and wholeness in the later years. Journal of Religious Gerontology, 7(1/2), 5-24.

The author notes the need for social gerontology to include theoretical and empirical contributions on the spiritual nature, needs, and resources of humanity. Currently, spiritual well-being has no precise, accepted definition. Two major paradigmatic orientations stand in contrast to each other: one stresses the explicit development of the self, the other views serving others and the "loss of self" as the means to attain spiritual maturity and self-fulfillment.

522. Moberg, D. O. (1984, June). Subjective measures of spiritual well-being. Review of Religious Research, 25, 351-364.

This article reports some exploratory efforts to consturct instruments for the measurement of spiritual well-being. Ten indices of SWB were developed, seven of which consist of items shown by factor analysis to cluster together. Although the measurement of SWB requires further research, SWB should not be ignored in the study of life satisfaction, wholistic well-being, and many areas of religious research.

523. Ruffing-Rahal, M. A. (1984, March/April). The spiritual dimension of well-being: Implications for the elderly. Home Healthcare Nurse, 2, 12-14.

A holistic model of health incorporates the spiritual dimension because of its contribution to personal well-being in the elderly. Spiritual experiences may enhance a self-perception that stresses the cumulative evaluation of a person over a lifetime, an integration of past and present into a meaningful unity. This provides a wellspring of personal strengths and healing energies against illness and adversity. The home health nurse plays a critical role in instituting holistic programs of health care.

524. Simmons, H. C. (1990, April). Religious instruction about aging and old age, (ERIC Document Reproduction Service No. ED 312 595).

This analysis of a variety of written resources to determine precise themes and motifs in religious instruction about aging and old age includes an analysis of literature using the term "spiritual well-being." Noted is the shift from an earlier affirmation of dependence on God and rootedness in a community of faith to a more generic and secular understanding of the term.

Dissertations

525. Fischbacher-McCrae, E. (1988/1989). The aging process for women: Focus on the influence of spirituality on adaptation (Doctor of Philosophy dissertation, The Union for Experimenting Colleges and Universities). DAI, 50, 712A.

This study tested the hypothesis that spirituality, as expressed in religious beliefs and practices, supports women's adaptation to the changes of post-middle life. The hypothesis was not confirmed.

526. Glicksman, A. (1990). The psychological well-being of elderly Jews: A comparative analysis (Doctor of Philosophy dissertation, University of Pennsylvania). DAI, 51, 2885A.

This study examined the relation of cultural (including religious and ethnic) background to responses on tests designed to measure psychological well-being. Two hypotheses were confirmed: that Jewish elderly would score significantly lower than other groups, and that even when holding constant the major determinants of psychological well-being Jewish status would continue to be a significant predictor of scores. The author concluded that cultural background has a significant effect on scores of tests intended to measure psychological well-being and that groups noted for expressive styles of behavior are likely to score lower than groups noted for more stoic styles of behavior.

527. Linz, R. (1990). <u>Meaning in old age</u> (Doctor of Philosophy dissertation, California School of Professional Psychology at Berkeley/Alameda). <u>DAI</u>, <u>51</u>, 3138B.

This study investigated whether spirituality (formal religious beliefs and personal ideals) had an effect on the aged individual's sense of physical well-being. The study concluded that healthy people who espouse spiritual values and who are active in religious life or activities (prayer, meditation, attending church) have a higher purpose in life.

Life Review and
Written Reminiscences

LIFE REVIEW

Books

528. Berry, T. (1982). Preface. In F. V. Tiso (Ed.), Aging: Spiritual perspectives (pp. 1-11). Lake Worth, FL: Sunday Publications.

In this major essay by a foremost commentator on ecology and spirituality, interreligious dialogue, and the wisdom of the planet, Berry locates the importance of the elderly in the human community in an extraordinary sequence of transformations in the entire earth process. Those who have lived through the changes of this century are in a privileged place to understand and to participate in "the vision of a post-industrial ecological age of intercommunion based on awareness of the inter-dependence of all the living and non-living forces of the planet" (p. 3). For Berry, the "wisdom of the elderly is carried not fundamentally in moralizations or in any philosophical or even religious principles but in the structure of their own being which finds its finest expression in their life stories" (p. 8).

529. Hateley, B. J. (1985). Telling your story, exploring your faith: Writing your life story for personal insight and spiritual growth. St. Louis, MO: CPB, 117p.

While intended for all ages, "the point of [this] book is to help you write your life story, and in the process to learn more about yourself, your faith, and your God" (p. 10). Older persons alone or in groups may use this book to write their life story; pastoral counselors may find it helpful in counseling and in training seminars.   Several writing exercises and sensitizing questions are included in each chapter.

530. Jenkins, S. (1978). Past present: Recording life stories of older people. Washington, DC: St. Alban's Parish, 149p.

This is mainly a book on how to listen to older people and how to expand listening into recording life histories.   Three interviews and photographs from the interviewees lives comprise most of the book.   A final chapter takes the reader step by step through the listening process and outlines a training program for volunteers.

531. Kaminsky, M. (Ed.). (1984). The uses of reminiscence: New ways of working with older adults [Special Issue].   Journal of Gerontological Social Work, 7(1/2).

This issue of The Journal of Gerontological Social Work presents a coherent and sophisticated conceptual understanding of reminiscence.   Several essays illustrate a variety of practical approaches for using reminiscence individually and in groups, to help participants accomplish a level of meaning which is personally integrative and socially critical.

Articles

532. Clements, W. M. (1981, Spring). Reminiscence as the cure of souls in early old age. Journal of Religion and Health, 20(1), 41-47.

This article considers the enhanced interest in the past of those in early old age. It suggests that reminiscence may provide an opportunity for recognizing and affirming positive values.   This is an important step in spiritual maturity or wholeness.   If reminiscence is shared it fits into the early Christian concept of "cure of souls".

533. Climo, J. J. (1989, Fall). Where volcanoes erupt: An oral narrative. The Journal of Aging and Judaism, 4, 53-63.

Using a specific oral narrative, the author explores themes of separation particularly relevant to the lives of early twentieth century immigrants, who are cut off both from the sources of childhood experience in another country and from their more Americanized children.

534. Georgemiller, R. J., & Getsinger, S. H. (1987). Reminiscence therapy: Effects on more and less religious elderly. Journal of Religion & Aging, 4(2), 47-58.

Life Review Workshops, consisting of seven weekly meetings of 90 minutes each, were conducted with 34 seniors. While essentially identical in age, education, and physical health, the more religious group reported a significantly higher level of intrinsically motivated religion and a more positive attitude toward death prior to the program. After the program the less religious group gained in purpose in life, became more religious, and denied less the prospect of death. No significant change in these areas occurred in the more religious group.

535. Gross, G. D. (1985, Spring). The spiritual lifeline: An experiential exercise. Journal of Religion & Aging, 1(3), 31-37.

Developed initially as a way for clergy to work with hospitalized elderly parishioners, the Spiritual Lifeline Exercise is presented as a way for elderly persons--or anyone curious about existential questions--to consider their spiritual growth. Steps for facilitating the exercise are given.

536. Guttmann, D. (1989, Summer). Hasidic teachings and logotherapy for the Jewish aged. The Journal of Aging and Judaism, 3, 173-185.

The author applies Hasidic teachings and Logotherapy to the task of helping older Jewish people in Jewish community centers, nursing and old age homes, attain ego integrity. The three pillars upon which Hasidic teachings rest are Intention, Service, and Enthusiasm. Intention refers to the realization that the intent of all deeds should be the perfection of the human spirit; Service refers to prayer with perfect devotion or service of others; and Enthusiasm means the kindling of a fire in the heart so that people may perform tasks with zest.

537. Haight, B. K. (1989). Life review: A method for pastoral counseling: Parts I and II. Journal of Religion & Aging, 5(3), 17-41.

The author describes a structured life review process in pastoral counseling which takes about six weeks to complete. In a series of studies conducted over six years it was found that those who completed the structured life review process indicated a higher level of life satisfaction than those that did not.

538. Holtzclaw, L. R. (1985, Spring). The importance of self-concept for the older adult. Journal of Religion & Aging, 1(3), 23-29.

This essay discusses the importance of a positive self-concept as a way for the older adult to transcend past experiences and integrate various roles in order to move toward self-actualization.

539. Kaminsky, M. (1987, Spring/Summer). A Legacy. The Journal of Aging and Judaism, 1, 166-170.

This powerful story of a women's relationship with her daughter as she records her own life story might be used in a program of oral history.

540. Kimble, M. A. (1990). Aging and the search for meaning. Journal of Religious Gerontology, 7(1/2), 111-130.

This article describes the process by which the meaning of aging can be interpreted using Viktor Frankl's meaning theory. The article is based on a conviction that individuals are motivated to find meaning throughout life and that self-transcendence is the essence of human existence.

541. Lantz, J., & Lantz, J. (1989). Meaning, tragedy and logotherapy with the elderly. Journal of Religion & Aging, 5(4), 43-51.

Elderly persons may experience tragic situations which the mental health practitioner is called upon to help resolve. This article stresses the importance of helping the elderly client experience, discover, and create meaning. Selected logotherapy intervention methods are described.

542. Leslie, R. C. (1982, Spring/Summer). Counseling the aged. International Forum for Logotherapy, 5(1), 47-52.

This article describes principles of logotherapy which individuals could use to prepare themselves for retirement, with which visitors to the old in nursing homes or hospitals could go beyond sympathetic listening, and with which groups of older persons could share experiences as experts on their own lives.

These techniques may encourage older people to accept their uniqueness, their capacity to make choices, and to find meaning in their lives up to the final hour.

543. Magee, J. J. (1987, Spring/Summer). Life review: A spiritual way for older adults. Journal of Religion & Aging, 3(3/4), 23-33.

This paper presents a model of integrative life review in three parts. The first component examines the family context of the life review and the pervasive effect of family context throughout the life cycle. The second component explains the role of confidants or groups in sharing memories, feelings, and self-assessments. The third component explores the way in which such a "companionate life review" may elicit and affirm more gratifying images of God.

544. Missinne, L. E., & Willeke-Kay, J. (1985, Summer). Reflections on the meaning of life in older age. Journal of Religion & Aging, 1(4), 43-58.

In this essay, four fundamental ideas of Viktor Frankl's theory concerning the meaning of life are applied to the behavior of older adults: 1) individuals create meaning in life through choices they are free to make, 2) one's values are important to the meaning of life, 3) each person has a responsibility for right action and right conduct, 4) the meaning of life consists of both ultimate and provisional meanings. Interviews with older persons are used to reflect on these concepts. Ministers and others working with older persons may find these concepts useful in relieving stress that may be more spiritual than psychological.

545. Randall, R. L. (1986, September). Reminiscing in the elderly: Pastoral care of self-narratives. The Journal of Pastoral Care, 40, 207-15.

Reminiscing in the elderly is interpreted within a self-psychology perspective. The author sees "self-narratives" as serving three psychological functions: 1) providing a continuity of the self, 2) sustaining a meaningful continuity of the self, and 3) uplifting the self through hope. Pastoral care can aid psychological development by: listening to life narratives; encouraging life narrations; and offering personal, religious interpretations to life narratives.

546. Richter, R. L. (1985, Fall/1985-86, Winter). Attaining ego integrity

through life review. Journal of Religion & Aging, 2(1/2), 1-11.

This article applies two theological ideas to Erikson's last stage of life, the crisis of ego integrity versus despair. They are 1) a review of life using James Fowler's idea of "master story" to connect effectively with cherished religious symbols, and 2) Donald Capp's idea of "parabolic event," which helps interpret past events for new insights.

547. Simmons, H. C. (1983). Strengthening personal support systems: Panelist's response. Alberta Symposium on Aging, 1982: Guidelines for the Future (pp. 76-78). Edmonton, Alberta, Canada: Alberta Social Services and Community Health.

These proceedings identify crucial tasks which the elderly must accomplish for themselves and for the broader human community. These are tasks of meaning, a personal integration for themselves and tasks of memory and wisdom for the human community--a life-review which is far greater than the story of any one individual.

548. Sukosky, D. G. (1989). Disengagement and life review: The possible relevance of integrating theological perspectives. Journal of Religion & Aging, 5(4), 1-14.

Some elderly find disengagement and life review useful in seeking fulfillment in old age. This article inquires about the possible theological relevance of the process of introspection. Five theological perspectives are proposed: 1) acknowledging the value of social withdrawal ("resignation before God"), 2) unconditional basis for self-worth, 3) freedom from guilt, 4) coming to terms with loss, and 5) the transformation of hope.

Dissertations

549. Kerins, M. R. (1985). The spiritual development of the older adult as related to the life review process (Doctor of Ministry thesis, Catholic University of America). DAI, 46, 1322A.

This project concludes with a program to facilitate the exploration of the spiritual life by an older adult in the context of life tasks of the later years. Robert Butler's life review theory is illustrated with writings from Teresa of Avila.

550. Rambaud, R. L. (1986). <u>Life stories of older adults: pastoral perspectives, pastoral evaluations and pastoral responses</u> (Unpublished Doctor of Ministry thesis, Boston University School of Theology).

This project uses theological themes taken from Elizabeth Whitehead and Paul Pruyser to view life stories of older adults. Resulting ministry is informed, intentional, and continuous in care.

551. Weintraub, R. L. (1988). <u>Telling is being: Creating meaning in old age</u> (Doctor of Philosophy dissertation, The University of Rochester). <u>DAI</u>, <u>49</u>, 2292A.

This dissertation studies the way in which participants in an adult day service program talk about their lives. It concludes that in choosing what to tell in their stories participants state who they are. Ethnicity and religion are salient features of identity and experience. The study points to a high level of heterogeneity among elders and recommends programs and policies which are adaptable to individual needs.

WRITTEN REMINISCENCES

Books

552. Boyle, S. (1983). <u>The desert blooms: A personal adventure in growing old creatively</u>. Nashville, TN: Abingdon, 207p.

This is a personal account of a professional woman's experiences with aging--the shocks, the despair, the adventure of recovery and becoming a new person. The role of faith, beliefs, and the church are woven throughout her account.

553. Davis, R. (1989). <u>My journey into Alzheimer's disease</u>. Wheaton, IL: Tyndale House, 140p.

This is an autobiographical account of the author's life after he was diagnosed as having Alzheimer's disease. It is a unique and very personal record of the physical, psychological, and spiritual changes that occured to one man living with this disease.

554. Guidice, L. (1973). The gift of retirement (D. Green, Trans.). Richmond, VA: John Knox, 64p.

Translated from German, this little book of short reflections has a poetic charm that is likely to spark a response. These personal reflections about just the first day of retirement could be used as a basis for meditations, for prayer, for discussion, or for a fresh look at life in retirement. At another level, this book could be a model for keeping a journal.

555. Hope, M. (1956). Towards evening: Reflections on growing old. London: Sheed & Ward, 178p.

This book is written as a journal over the course of one year by a prominent English Catholic author as part of the series "Prayer and Practice." While the text is both local and dated, this book might serve as a model for journaling by seniors who want to record both their "hearts" and their wisdom.

556. Lee-Hostetler, J. (1988). Seasons of change. Elgin, IL: Brethern Press, 186p.

Louisa Nussbaum Hochsletler Basinger, the great-grandmother of the author, reveals in story form her transition to life in a nursing home. Throughout the story, Louisa, a Mennonite, reveals how her strong faith in God that gave her strength throughout her life now makes her able to adjust to the impersonal routine of nursing home life.

557. Murphy, C. (1989). Milestone 70. Wallingford, PA: Pendle Hill, 39p.

This, the author's seventeenth Pendle Hill Pamphlet, is a series of brief reflections in the form of journal entries written during her seventy-first year, exploring the texture of her daily life. It might be used as a model for a year-long journal.

558. Pierskalla, C. S. (1992). Rehearsal for retirement: My journey into the future. Valley Forge, PA: National Ministries, American Baptist Churches, USA, 92p.

This journal is in two parts. "The Journey" is about the month the author spent in the Midwest, living alone on a fixed income, "like an old lady." "Winter Sabbath" contains the author's reflections from her shore retreat. While the book is very personal, it is set up to invite the reader's reflections and to draw out implications for ministry.

559. Scott-Maxwell, F. (1979). The measure of my days. New York: Alfred A. Knopf (Original copyright 1968), 150p.

This is a book of extraordinarily perceptive personal reflections on aging written at age 82 by an author and Jungian psychologist who views herself growing more passionate and intense with age. These reflections began as a notebook she used for asking and answering her own questions.

Articles

560. Cole, T. R., & Premo, T. (1986-87). The pilgrimage of Joel Andrews: Aging in the autobiography of a Yankee farmer. International Journal of Aging and Human Development, 24(2), 79-85.

Using excerpts from an autobiography, the authors portray one ordinary man's struggle with aging and death within the context of his own history and religious beliefs. In a fourteen month pilgrimage, away from, and, it would appear, estranged from family, he undergoes the religiously sanctioned transition from physical man to spiritual man. Of note is his evangelistic outreach and the satisfaction it gave him.

561. Leeser, I. (1989, Summer). "Readings for the Old" from The Occident. The Journal of Aging and Judaism, 3, 203-209.

The Occident published a short series of "Readings for the Old" in alternating issues beginning July 1851. Some themes which emerge in the three reproduced in this article are preparation for the journey into eternity by a retrospect of the past, by actions, and by example; a self-examination on our relationships with our parents; and a review of adult life including commercial and business practice, seeking after treasure, observance of the Sabbath, and relationship with spouse. "Our wife too! Oh, pardon thou patient participator of all our former sufferings and deprivations, thou venerable partner of our present peaceful and tranquil happiness, for thus recalling to your mind our former sinful course to you; how did we neglect your wise counsel! [...] how did we slight your pure and holy example..." (p. 208).

562. Rogal, S. J. (1987).   John Wesley's eighty-seventh year: Good is the work of the Lord. Journal of Religion & Aging, 4(1), 67-77.

A study of Wesley's journals, diaries, and letters from the last 14 months of his life show a man who had come to his physical end without any diminishment of his evangelistic fervor.

Dissertations

563. Premo, T. L. (1983).   Women growing old in the new republic: Personal responses to old age, 1785-1835 (Doctor of Philosophy dissertation, University of Cincinnati). DAI, 44, 1897A.

This work studies the personal responses to growing old of 142 white, middle and upper-class Protestant women in the 50 years following American independence.   Continuity dominated the lives of aging women, yet they preferred independent living arrangements and enjoyed strong emotional attachments with other females.   Older women also found comfort in strong religious foundations which reinforced the view of aging as a cycle of ripening, decay, and rebirth.   In the moral sphere, women became models of piety for younger generations, strengthening the classical view of aging.   Disengagement and resignation, the keys to salvation at the end of life, often proved difficult. This study raises serious questions about D. H. Fischer's contention that in post-Revolutionary America old people lost esteem.

Death and Dying

Books

564. Adams, J. R. <u>The sting of death: A study course on death and bereavement</u>. New York: Seabury, 94p.

This leader's guide for a study course on death and bereavement notes that older people are, for the most part, willing to talk about death. A six-session course may be used either with a small study group or as a program for an entire parish. The course focuses on death and bereavement from a variety of perspectives--biblical, societal, practical.

565. Congdon, H. K. (1977). <u>The pursuit of death</u>. Nashville, TN: Abingdon, 191p.

This engaging philosophical work pursues death both as a metaphysical and an existential event. Although the author does not connect death and age, this book could be used with seniors who wish to face this compelling subject. In probing the mysteries of death he is "probing into the very bowels of our being. We are dying" (p. 14). Chapters include: "Some Problems," "Toward a Definition of Death," "The Soul," "Death as a Uniquely Human Event," "God-Talk," "Ego Death," "Immortality," "Confronting Death".

566. Green, P. (1950). <u>Old age and the life to come: A book for old people</u>. London: A. R. Mowbray, 64p.

This little book has a certain distinctiveness in devotional literature about old age. It addresses three questions: What should be the plans and provisions for the last stages of the journey? How is life's close to be faced, and in what spirit? What do we believe about the life to come and on what warrant?

567. Kastenbaum, R. (Ed.).   (1987, Spring).   Death and bereavement. Generations, 11(3).

In this issue on death and bereavement, Robert Kastenbaum emphasizes in his essay "The Search for Meaning," that while death and dying are no longer taboo subjects, "healthcare givers still enact rituals of evasion and distancing when the shadow of death challenges their sense of control" (p. 9). Other essays focus on a look at the consequences of viewing death in old age as more natural than death at an earlier age (Sally Gadow); hospice philosophy and practice (Jean Taylor); invaluable role of countertransference to both client and helper (Renee Katz and Bonnie Genevay); sources of grief (Richard Kalish); the Navajo view of death (Ken White); suicide among the old (Nancy Osgood).

568. Lewis, C. S. (1961). A grief observed. Minneapolis: Seabury Press, 60p.

This small book is the author's account of the meaning of his wife's death, recorded in longhand in several notebooks, his bereavement as a way of dealing with it. The author questions his beliefs about God and reveals his indecision and self-pity.

569. Mount, B. M. (1983). Sightings. Downers Grove, IL: InterVarsity, 126p.

Although the author is a medical doctor and leader in Canada's death awareness movement, this book is not a case study but a poetic reflection on the death of his mother. These reflections on the joys and sorrows of life written from a Christian perspective were a response to his mother's request for something to read.

570. Murphy, M. (1988). New images of the last things: Karl Rahner on death and life after death. New York: Paulist, 96p.

This theological treatise explains one theologian's understanding of death and life after death, compares it with the teaching of the Roman Catholic Church, and develops an American theology of death. [Books of this genre are included in this section only if the author makes specific reference to death in old age or if the treatise is included in a book or collection on aging.].

571. Sullender, R. S. (1989). Losses in later life: A new way of walking with God. New York: Paulist Press, 183p.

A Presbyterian minister and pastoral counselor sensitively discusses the major losses that occur in the second half of life: loss of youth, family, parents, work, spouse, health, and identity. He views these losses as different from losses earlier in life because they are more frequent, often permanent, and usually not growth experiences. Grieving these losses and finding new identities and spiritual meanings is the challenge. According to the author, psychological health is dependent upon being able to grieve well.

Articles

572. Atwood, D. B. (1983, Spring). Death and dying in the local parish. Reformed Review, 36, 108-149.

This article outlines a complete course on death and dying which the author taught in a local hospital. Six sessions of one hour each are presented along with a list of resources.

573. Baum, R. C. (1982). A revised interpretive approach to the religious significance of Death in Western Societies. Sociological Analysis, 43(4), 327-350.

This article attempts a more systematically ordered interpretation of death in the modern West through a perusal of prominent contemporary theological writing on the meaning of suffering and death and through a critical review of a tendency toward one-function reductionism of the work of Parsons on the meaning of death in modern society. The author notes the "remarkable difference between Catholic and Protestant death theology with respect to religious obligations in dying" (p.347). Catholics have a far greater emphasis on individualism and activism; Protestant positions suggest meek submission to death.

574. Fastiggi, R. (1982). Aging, death and the after life. In F. V. Tiso

(Ed.), Aging: Spiritual perspectives (pp. 221-248). Lake Worth, FL: Sunday Publications.

This study concludes that death is a deep mystery and that "we approach the dark road towards death with nothing to guide us--except some hopes, fears and a vague but profound trust in the loving powers that be" (p. 219).

575. Gainer, J. A. (1987). Voices from the dark. Journal of Religion & Aging, 4(2), 83-99.

The author presents a portrait of two real people who struggle against suffering and dying and in that reveal something about that which lasts.

576. Halper, T. (1979, Spring). On death, dying, and terminality: Today, yesterday, and tomorrow. Journal of Health Politics, Policy and Law, 4(1), 11-29.

The author sees a shift in the perception of death from fear and hostility to sentimentality and trivialization. He suggests that the hospice movement may provide physical and emotional amelioration of suffering.

577. Kalish, R. A., & Reynolds, D. K. (1977). The role of age in death attitudes. Death Education, 1, 205-230.

This article reports a study of 434 adults, equally divided among four ethnic groups, among women and men, and among three age categories. Consistent with other studies, this research found that older persons were least likely to indicate fear of their own death. The elderly had also encountered significantly more deaths and attended significantly more funerals, but they also thought about their own dying and death.

578. Lund, D. A., Caserta, M. S., & Ellor, J. W. (1988). A comparison of bereavement adjustments between Mormon and non-Mormon older adults. Journal of Religion & Aging, 5(1/2), 75-92.

This article reports a study of 190 bereaved persons, ages 50 to 93, at three time periods (3 weeks, 1 year and 2 years). Mormons (73% of the sample) were slightly more religious and active and had slightly larger support networks than the non-Mormons. Nevertheless, the two groups did not differ on any of the ten measures of adjustment.

579. Matt, H. J. (1987, Winter). Fading image of God? Theological reflections of a nursing home chaplain. Judaism: A Quarterly Journal of Jewish Life and Thought, 36(1), 75-83.

The author inquires about the relationship between the image of God and the human body (created in the image of God), as that body is observed to deteriorate. He affirms that the body is, no matter at what stage of deterioration, still the image of God. Finally he affirms that there is basis in traditional Jewish teaching for ultimate hope beyond the grave in the restoration of the soul to the body.

580. Pherigo, L. P. (1986, Fall/Winter). Death: The inevitable issue. Journal of Religion & Aging, 3(1/2), 63-73.

The author concludes that our understanding of death as release of the soul (spirit, self) from the non-essential self will continue, that more will die at home than in hospital, and that we will probably learn some new things about death from the new physics and from psychic research. In the same issue, W. Paul Jones challenges eight primary theories of aging in contemporary United States culture. He suggests that the image of elders is a symbolic reminder of death. This results in their rejection or departmentalization through invisibility. This, in turn, is the dynamic known as ageism.

581. Rosik, C. H. (1989). The impact of religious orientation in conjugal bereavement among older adults. International Journal of Aging and Human Development, 28, 251-260.

In a study of the relationship between religious commitment and adaptation to widowhood (n=159) it was found that for this sample extrinsicness was highly correlated with greater grief and depression. The direction of causality was not definitely established.

582. Saiving, V. C. (1988, Fall). Our bodies/our selves: Reflections on sickness, aging, and death. Journal of Feminist Studies in Religion, 4, 117-125.

In this essay, the author reflects on the finitude of the body not only as it is expressed in the aging process but by people of all ages through pain, illness, disability, and death.

583. Scott, N. A. (1973).   The modern imagination of death.   In J. D. Roslansky (Ed.), The end of life: A discussion at the Nobel Conference (pp. 39-48). Amsterdam: North-Holland.

Scott suggests that the relocation of the problem of death from the dimension of eternity to the dimension of time may to some extent render the modern imagination, as discovered in literature, more open to what is the real heart of the Christian hope for human destiny. For Scott, human destiny is understood in terms of the redemption of the body.

584. Spero, M. H. (1982, Summer). Reflections on the inevitability of death: A Jewish existential approach. Judaism: A Quarterly Journal of Jewish Life and Thought, 31, 333-345.

This article deals with the intersection between halakhic and psychological views on the confrontation with dying and death, with a focus on how Jewish rabbinic thinking sought to prepare the individual throughout a lifetime for this confrontation.   Aging is conceptualized as nearness to death, calling for self-transcendence rather than self-actualization. This reinforces a continuous life-review.   Repentance signifies ultimate personal creativity and spiritual heroism.

585. Stendahl, K. (1973).   Immortality is too much and too little. In J. D. Roslansky (Ed.), The end of life: A discussion at the Nobel Conference (pp. 73-83). Amsterdam: North-Holland.

The issue of the end of life is the mystery of the will of God for God's creation rather than for the individual. Human beings, who suffer from the problem of over-power, should take a lower posture and let go of a certain fighting arrogance which projects human importance into immortality. "The search for identity perpetuation or immortality as assurance should be lifted out of the ego and be placed in God" (p. 83).

586. Studzinski, R. (1987).   Impasse, finitude, and guilt: Some religious challenges of aging. Bulletin of the Menninger Clinic, 51, 436-446.

The author offers responses from writers in the Western Christian tradition to dilemmas the elderly face (impasse--feeling stuck or powerless, finitude, and guilt over past mistakes and failures). Religious responses to these crises may provide a renewed sense of meaning and direction for elderly persons.

Dissertations

587. Feinson, M. C. (1982/1983). Distress and social support: A needs assessment of bereaved older adults (Doctor of Philosophy dissertation, Rutgers University). DAI, 43, 3432A.

This study of 163 bereaved individuals indicates that distress is not significantly related to socio-demographic characteristics such as age, income, education, length of bereavement, and number of stressful life events. Thirty-six percent of widows' distress is explained by two health and three social support variables. Health perceptions account for 31%. In contrast, health variables do not explain any of the widowers' distress. Three social support measures, religious preference, and employment status account for 42% of widowers' distress.

588. O'Laughlin, K. S. (1981). Elderly people's attitudes toward death: Empirical and experiential evidence (Doctor of Education dissertation, Boston University School of Education). DAI, 42, 2508B.

This study investigated the attitudes toward death and dying (of self and others) held by an urban population in an elderly housing complex. It tested the efficacy of a series of five workshops (in which participants discussed aging, loss, and death in relation to their values and philosophies) aimed at decreasing fear of death.

589. Sornberger, J. A. (1986). Open Heart (Doctor of Philosophy dissertation [original poetry], The University of Nebraska). DAI, 47, 2580A.

The first of six sections of original poetry in this collection concerns itself with doubt, hope, and the uncertainty surrounding death. The speaker examines her religious heritage and her inability to fully accept what it offers.

590. Thekkedam, J. K. (1981). A cross-cultural study of death anxiety and religious belief (Doctor of Philosophy dissertation, St. Louis University)

DAI, 42, 4214B.

This study concluded that whereas cultural facts seem to facilitate the reduction of death anxiety in India, it is the intensity of religious belief that is operative in lessening death fear in the USA. Subjects in both countries included both Jesuit seminarians and lay male Catholics.

Theology, Bible, and Other Religions

THEOLOGY

Books

591. Bianchi, E. C. (1984). Aging as a spiritual journey. New York: Crossroad, 285p.

A study of the dilemmas posed for the human spirit by the realities of aging and death, the religious basis of this book is broadly Christian with occasional excursions into Judaism and Eastern religions. This work is strongly influenced by Jungian psychology.

592. Blythe, R. (1979). The view in winter: Reflections on old age. New York: Penguin Books, 270p.

The author interviews older people from many walks of life: farmer, miner, war veteran, schoolteacher, clergyman, actor, engineer and others. The result is an inquiring and reflective essay that touches the depths of a human condition often ignored.

593. Clements, W. M. (Ed.). (1981). Ministry with the aging. San Francisco, CA: Harper & Row, 274p.

This is a collection of 16 essays under the headings of foundations, challenges, designs by theologians, social scientists, philosophers, psychologists, and medical doctors.

594. Fischer, K. (1985). Winter grace. New York: Paulist Press, 170p.

The author, a Roman Catholic theologian and counselor, shows how Christian faith can transform the later years of life. Fischer presents an inclusive definition of spirituality as "the ultimate ground of all our questions, hopes, fears, and loves: our efforts to deal creatively with retirement and to find a purpose for our lives after our family has been raised; our struggles with the loss of a spouse or the move from a home of many years; questions of self-worth and fear of reaching out to make new friendships; the discovery of new talents, deeper peace, wider boundaries of love" (p. 9). Chapters deal with memories, dependence and independence, love and sexuality, humor and hope, loss, dying and resurrection. Of particular note is the chapter on "Older Women" with the lives of several biblical women used to illuminate the experiences of many older women.

595. Freeman, C. B. (1979). The senior adult years: A Christian psychology of aging. Nashville, TN: Broadman Press, 204p.

Freeman presents a theological context for viewing demographics; psychological functions, needs, and adjustment; and development, disorders, and implications. Readers are encouraged to see both the positive and negative aspects of aging.

596. Harton, S. (1957). On growing old: A book of preparation for age. New York: Morehouse-Gorham, 126p.

This book (which precedes the pop devotional texts of the 1960s and 1970s) probes the declines of old age and death within the context of a thoughtful, mature, and ultimately demanding theodicy. The author considers the anatomy of suffering and the assignment of evil. In the context of Christian faith she sees that the last years have a "vital and grand purpose and an essential work of their own" (p. 7). Selected chapter headings indicate the scope of this work: suffering; an analysis of evil; the Savior; Christ and suffering; the treasury of pain; the trials of old age; the glory of death.

597. Hendricks, W. L. (1986). A theology for aging. Nashville, TN: Broadman, 300p.

This book assumes that seniors have insights into Bible and theology that are of value for the wider Christian community. At the same time, normative

Christian theology has relevance for the senior adult who is coping with physical, emotional and financial realities that are often difficult to accept or understand. The experiences of normal, everyday life are used as metaphors to express the content of theology. This book assumes the authority of God through Scripture and reflects a conservative, Protestant, conversional perspective.

598. Kao, C. C. L. (Ed.). (1988). <u>Maturity and the quest for spiritual meaning</u>. Lanham, MD: University Press of America, 211p.

This is a collection of papers originally presented at two symposia: "Maturity, Spirituality and Theological Reconstruction" and "Maturity in Ministry," sponsored by Maturity Studies Institute, Inc. All papers explore the idea of the spiritual meaning of life. The work is divided into three parts: Foundations of Meaning-Making; Life and Crises of Meaning-Making; and Maturity and Meaningful Ministry.

599. LeFevre, C., & LeFevre, P. (Eds.). (1985). <u>Aging and the human spirit</u>. Chicago, IL: Exploration, 374p.

This reader in religion and gerontology contains 37 reprinted essays written in the 1970s and early 1980s. Essays are organized under these topics: aging in the Western religious tradition, religion and aging in contemporary theology, facts and myths of aging, social science research, policy and program, and ministry to the aged.

600. Lyon, K. B. (1985). <u>Toward a practical theology of aging</u>. Philadelphia, PA: Fortress, 128p.

The relationship of human fulfillment and aging is foundational to pastoral care with older adults and forms the core of the discussion in this volume. The author critically probes the claims of historic theological literature on older adulthood as well as contemporary theological and psychological interpretations of experience to produce a practical theological understanding of old age.

601. Missinne, L. E. (1990). <u>Reflections on aging: A spiritual guide</u>. Liguori, MO: Liguori, 112p.

This book reflects on some fundamental questions of human existence in older age: meaning, suffering, purpose of living, Christian spirituality, aging, dying. Its particular emphasis is on the discovery of personal meaning in older age, and on the witness to the young of how much meaning and value older life can have.

Articles

602. Brewer, E. D. C. (1986, Fall/Winter). Research in religion and aging: An unlikely scenario. Journal of Religion & Aging, 3(1/2), 91-102.

The author notes the need to build theoretical/theological models around meaningful research, and presents one such model. He then notes three areas for research: nature and role of spirituality in the lives of the elderly, the role of organized religion in quality aging, and the relation of these and other areas of research to the aging process and to culture, society, and the physical world.

603. Browning, D. S. (1975, Winter). Preface to a practical theology of aging. Pastoral Psychology, 24, 151-81.

The author reflects on Erikson's concept of generativity in order to develop a theology of aging. A practical theology of aging must take seriously the phenomenon of aging as well as empirical analyses; it must place all this in conversation with Christian symbols. He argues that the key to meaningful aging is learning to care for oneself, one's future, and the future of the race.

604. Curran, C. E. (1982). A theological perspective on aging. In Moral theology: A continuing journey (pp. 93-111). Notre Dame, IN: University of Notre Dame.

The author questions the validity of a slope or peak view of human existence. He puts in its place a Christian view of death and life as interpreted through the pascal mystery. The believing Christian sees death as a way to the fullness of life. "The old and the old-old should be truly active in the most personal sense of being active--giving meaning and intelligibility to their lives. For the Christian the meaning comes in terms of the living out of the paschal mystery by which we come to know and experience the Lord in the fellowship of his suffering and in the power of his resurrection" (p. 106).

605. Dahlstrom, E. C. (1979, February). Toward a theology of aging. Covenant Quarterly, 37, 3-15.

The author uses six central areas of theological concern to reflect upon a Christian theology of aging: time, creation (life and death), man (personhood), vocation (purpose), salvation (love), and hope. He believes that a sound theological rationale is necessary as a foundation to any practical ministry with older adults.

606. Folkman, J. (1989, Fall). The ages of man in Jewish literature. The Journal of Aging and Judaism, 4, 27-37.

This article gives a variety of biblical and talmudic statements about aging. The actual texts are presented. In another article in this issue, Steven Reuben lists references (only) to a variety of biblical and Rabbinic text, indicating positive and negative attitudes.

607. Heinecker, M. J., & Hellerich, R. R. (1976). The church's ministry with older adults: A theological basis. New York: Lutheran Church in America, 27p.

This study guide is in three parts: Part I gives the theological affirmations and orientation; Part II is a guide for study and discussion; and Part III describes the Consulting Committee on Aging for the Lutheran Church in America.

608. Hiltner, S. (Ed.). (1975). Toward a theology of aging: A special issue of pastoral psychology. New York: Human Sciences Press, 181p.

The editor emphasized the unique opportunity and obligation of theology in relation to aging in serving as chairman of a Conference on Aging in 1974. The writers "make an earnest effort to discern the psychological, socio-historical, and theological meanings of aging in human life".

609. Jones, W. P. (1986, Fall/Winter). Theology and aging in the 21st century. Journal of Religion & Aging, 3(1/2), 17-32.

The author contrasts futuring as bourgeoisie projection--a simple extrapolation from the present--with futuring as normative forecasting--where the future is in paradoxical relation with the present. The future of aging from a theological perspective must follow the latter notion. Issues considered include the elderly as expendable, the aged and economic distribution, world tensions and age polarity, vocation as pilgrimage, the aged as electoral factor, compartmentalization and holism, the new leisure, spiritualization and the aging process, and creative models for an experimental future. In the same issue, James Thorson and Bruce Horacek observed that the plight of older persons in the future will require an intentional ministry which addresses feelings of self-esteem, value, and identity. Robert E. Buxbaum identifies four needs for adequate preparation for the pastoral care of the aged: training in group process, skills in conflict resolution, a theology of aging that is grounded in grace rather than works, and actual involvement with the elderly. John H. Lindquist reports on the movement of the "Boomer" generation toward old age and the need of churches to prepare.

610. Kragnes, E. N. (1981, May 13). Insights for the later years. The Christian Century, 98, 533-534.

A theology of aging is best located in the wisdom tradition. The author briefly develops four elements: the presence of God is order, not act; the purpose of human existence is life; weight should be placed on human freedom and responsibility; and, fullness of human life is God's present intention, not an endpoint of salvation history.

611. Richard, L. (1982). Toward a theology of aging. Science et Esprit, 34, 269-287.

The author proposes a political theology of aging seeking to transform the oppression of the elderly in a particular cultural context (ageism which makes dependency negative, leading to self-loss). Christian faith must free itself from an on-going tendency to see the Gospel from a triumphalistic perspective and embrace a theology based on Kenosis (the self-emptying and self-giving that is love's essence). "Commitment to the crucified involves a radical conversion and brings about a revolution in life" (p. 281). For successful aging we must free ourselves from a functional ethic which suggests that self-worth depends on economic and social performance.

Dissertations

612. Au, T. H. (1975). The church's role in the problem of aging (Doctor of Religion thesis, School of Theology at Claremont). DAI, 36, 3777A.

The author seeks to help in the rediscovery of a valued place for the aged in modern society through a critical theological inquiry into the nature of the foundations of society. Examined are notions of the value system implied in "usefulness" and in current attitudes about aging. Renewed conceptions about God may support an expanded spiritual awareness and new life styles. The role of the church as a supportive transition agent is explored.

613. Wechsler, H. J. (1982). Broken tablets in the ark: A study of the ideas of aging in Rabbinic literature (Doctor of Philosophy dissertation, The Graduate School of The Jewish Theological Seminary of America). DAI, 43, 483A.

This study examines ideas about aging, the process of aging, and the treatment of the old found in Rabbinic literature. The study first focuses on language used to refer to old age, then examines the experience of aging (physical and psychological). Finally the response in Rabbinic theology to the aging human body is examined, along with the commandments to stand before the old and to honor one's parents.

BIBLE

Books

614. Dulin, R. Z. (1988). A crown of glory: A biblical view of aging. New York: Paulist, 145p.

Dulin presents a phenomenological study of aging in the Hebrew scriptures based on these major themes: length of days, physical and psychological characteristics of aging, the old in the community, and old age as a time for human reflection. For the most part, the author has avoided present-day interpretation of historical meanings.

615. Harris, J. G. (1987). Biblical perspectives on aging. Philadelphia, PA: Fortress, 144p.

This historical-critical study of the elderly in the Bible recognizes that the Bible itself had no direct interest in the question of the elderly and thus draws conclusions on rather indirect and unintentional evidence. This work has a strong ethical component that concerns social process, social practice, and social value.

616. Sapp, S. (1987). <u>The full years: Aging and the elderly in the Bible and today</u>. Nashville, TN: Abingdon Press, 197p.

The author discusses both contemporary views of aging and the views of the Old and New Testaments in an attempt to more clearly define our obligation to the elderly today.

617. Stagg, F. (1981).   <u>The Bible speaks on aging</u>.   Nashville, TN: Broadman, 192p.

The author, a retired professor of New Testament Interpretation at the Southern Baptist Theological Seminary, studies age, aging and agism in each book of the Bible from Genesis through Revelation.   These interpretive and reflective writings are orgainized into chapters for persons using the book in a church setting: Pentateuch, Historical Books, Wisdom Books, Prophets, Synoptic Gospels and Acts, Johannine writings, Pauline writings, and General Epistles.

Articles

618. Bailey, L. R. (1989, Winter). Biblical perspectives on aging. <u>Quarterly Review: A Scholarly Journal for Reflection on Ministry</u>, <u>9</u>(4), 48-64.

This article approaches aging as a horrifying problem for the individual, for which there is little biblical wisdom. Where the author appeals to the Bible, there seems little which is applicable to the present situation. This article might form the basis for a case-study on attitudes toward aging.

619. Dulin, R. Z. (1986, Fall/Winter). The elderly in biblical society. <u>The Journal of Aging and Judaism</u>, <u>1</u>, 49-56.

This article describes a biblical view of aging from physiological, psychological, and sociological perspectives. The Bible helps us understand issues of aging because of its universal message and pragmatic view of life. Examples given in the Bible fuel human reflection on aging and one's conduct toward the elderly. The plea of the psalmist "cast me not off in old age" is the eternal voice of humanity.

620. Fox, M. V. (1988). Aging and death in Qohelet 12. Journal for the Study of the Old Testament, 42, 55-77.

This article studies the interplay among literal, symbolic, and figurative dimensions of Qohelet 12 ("And remember the Creator in the days of your youth [...] All is absurdity"), seeking to bring out scenes, connotations, and implications. The interpretation focuses on the primary effects the poem is intended to have on the reader, namely to connect the sense of fear with thoughts of one's own death. "After all, Qohelet says quite clearly that this is what lies ahead for you" (p. 71).

621. Larue, G. A. (1979). Biblical mythology and aging. In L. H. Sterns (Ed.), Gerontology in higher education: Developing institutions and community strength (pp. 81-90). Belmont, CA: Wadsworth.

The author considers the work ethic and retirement, biblical mythology and the life span, and biblical mythology and respect for elders. He concludes with a section on potentials for a new mythic emphasis and new ethic for aging.

622. Stagg, F. (1978). Biblical perspectives on aging. Athens, GA: General Assembly Mission Board (PCUS), and National Interfaith Coalition on Aging (NICA), 15p.

This article-length pamphlet addresses current perceptions of aging with what the author sees as relevant biblical messages: length of life, worth of persons, wisdom of age, maturity, care of the aged, euthanasia, retirement, affirming life in its full cycle. The author does not deal with biblical perspectives on aging on their own terms.

Dissertations

623. Anderson, D. E. (1990). Retire or refire? Goals for the final lap from Philippians (Doctor of Ministry thesis, Biola University, Talbot School of Theology). DAI, 51, 1258A.

This project is a verse-by-verse exposition, in a popular style, of the letter to the Philippians. Its aims are to challenge seniors into active ministry and Christian growth and to prepare them for the adjustments and losses of aging and retirement.

624. Reeder, H. L. (1981). <u>Responsibility for the elderly in light of Jewish literature</u> (Doctor of Ministry thesis, School of Theology at Claremont). <u>DAI</u>, <u>42</u>, 1680A.

This project studies the elderly in the Bible and Jewish tradition and develops a Jewish perspective on the care of the elderly. Three homes for the aged are studied (Jewish, Christian, nonsectarian), with interviews of 10 residents.

OTHER RELIGIONS

Books

625. Boskey, J. B., Hughes, S. C., Manley, R. H., & Wimmer, D. H. (1982). <u>Teaching about aging</u>. Washington, DC: University Press of America, 177p.

Part One, "A Model Curriculum on Religions and Aging," treats religions and aging in historical pespective (primitive religions, Hinduism, Buddhism, religions in China, the Ancient Near East, the Old Testament, Judaism, early Christianity, Islam). [This is followed by a treatment of] religions and aging in contemporary perspective. It deals with religion more on a social science basis than within denominational or religious-tradition perspectives.

626. Clements, W. (Ed.). (1988). Religion, aging and health: A global perspective. <u>Journal of Religion & Aging</u>, <u>4</u>(3/4).

This issue contains reflections on religion, aging, and health from seven religious perspectives: "Islam and the Health of the Elderly" by Hakim Mohammed Said; "Add Life to Years the Buddhist Way" by Daw Khin Myo Chit; "Judaism: Lifestyles Leading to Physical, Mental, and Social Wellbeing in Old Age" by A. Michael Davies; "The Teachings of Confucianism on Health and Old Age" by Takehiko Okada; "Catholicism, Lifestyles, and the Wellbeing of the Elderly" by Carmen Barros; "On Perennial Youth and Longevity: A Taoist View on Health of the Elderly" by Fumimaso Fukui; and "A Study of the Health of the Elderly from the Standpoint of Shinto" by Takeshi Mitsuhashi.

627. Kramer, K. (Ed.). (1988). <u>The sacred art of dying</u>. Mahwah, NJ: Paulist Press, 226p.

Focusing primarily on religious attitudes toward death, dying and afterlife, this book presents the story of death in its comparative religious context. Attitudes toward death of Hindus, Buddhists, Chinese, Jews, Christians, and Muslims are examined as well as reincarnation and resurrection, confession, conversion and confirmation.

628. Tiso, F. V. (Ed.). (1982). Aging: Spiritual perspectives. Lake Worth, FL: Sunday Publications, 256p.

In response to the U.N. General Assembly's appeal to non-governmental organizations, Opera Pia International (OPI) undertook a major consultation on aging from a variety of religious perspectives. OPI is convinced that the psychological and spiritual needs of older adults must be emphasized, their latent resources recognized and shared, and that the elderly are bearers of the fulness of life within human existence. Nine chapters on aging in the world's religions include "Knowledge is Power, but Age is Wisdom: The Challenge of Active Aging from an African Perspective" by Kofi Appiah-Kubi; "Aging Among Native Americans: The Quest for Wisdom" by John A. Grimm; "The Elderly and Moral Precepts in Chinese Tradition" by Albert Chi-Lu Chung; "The Place and Role of the Aged in the Hindu Perspective" by John B. Chethimattam; "Buddhism and Aging" by Buddhasa P. Kirthisinghe; "Aging: The Jewish Perspective" by Asher Finkel; "A Christian Theology of Aging" by Jose Pereira; "The Art of Aging According to the Monastic Tradition" by M. C. Cymbalista and Jean Leclercq; "The Aging in Islam" by Muhammad Abdul-Rauf.

Articles

629. Elias, J. (1988). Religious education of older adults: Historical perspectives. Educational Gerontology, 14, 269-267.

This article presents selected religious themes (Jewish, Christian, Confucian, and other) relevant to emerging efforts in the religious education of older adults. The author notes the encouragement of religious traditions for study and contemplation as appropriate activities for their older members.

630. Lecso, P. A. (1989). Aging through Buddhist eyes. Journal of Religion & Aging, 5(3), 59-66.

This article presents representative depictions of aging mainly from the Tibetan Buddhist literature. Their context indicates that they are not negative or pessimistic; rather they are meant to counter the conceit of youth and to act as spurs to spiritual growth and realization.

631. Liu, D. (1978).   Health and longevity in the wisdom of ancient China. In The Tao of health and longevity (pp. 10-33). New York: Shocken Books.

Health and longevity in Taoism and Confucianism are discussed in this chapter. To illustrate the ideas involved, the author quotes a number of passages from Lao Tzu and Confucius.

632. Luhmann, F. J. (1987, Spring/Summer). Respect for older persons: A Confucian perspective. Journal of Religion & Aging, 3(3/4), 83-90.

This article traces the Confucian tradition of respect for older persons, with its cultural and ethical basis, through 2000 years of Korean history.

633. Rudin, M. R. (1981, October). New target of the cults. 50 Plus, 20-23.

This article reports on the efforts of religious cults to recruit older people. Among these cults are the Unification Church, the Church Universal and Triumphant, the International Society for Krishna Consciousness, the Way International, and the Children of God. Older people are often urged to join in order to set an example to the younger generation. Recruitment is heaviest in Florida and California, but widows and lonely or discontented older people throughout the country may be receptive to proselytizers.

634. Weaver, R. C. (1987, Spring). A Gandhian model of health: Looking at Alzheimer's disease. Journal of Religion and Health, 26(1), 43-49.

This paper develops a model of health based on the ideas of Mahatma Gandhi. These are then applied to persons with Alzheimer's disease. From this is derived a program of simple meditation techniques and the use of the Mantram for individuals with mild, recently diagnosed Alzheimer's disease in order to enable these people to calm their minds and conserve their vital energy. Pre- and post-testing are part of this experiment.

Dissertations

635. Schemper, T. L. (1987/1988). <u>Aging, religion, and mastery style among the Quechua of Pocona, Bolivia</u> (Doctor of Philosophy dissertation, Northwestern University). <u>DAI</u>, <u>48</u>, 2477B.

This study evaluated the effects of age on subjective religious experiences and behaviors of the Quechua (in a traditional agricultural society). Older Quecha showed a greater sense of closeness to God. There were no age differences in belief in an afterlife. Old and young Quechua attributed different meanings to the same rituals.

636. Tilak, S. (1988). <u>Religion and aging in Indian tradition</u> (Doctor of Ministry thesis, McGill University [Canada]). <u>DAI</u>, <u>50</u>, 172A.

This study finds images and ideas of aging in selected Buddhist and Hindu texts. It studies their historical, semantic, and metaphysical dimensions. The study concludes that the bond between traditional Indian values of life (aging, stages of life, time, change, determinate actions, desire, and revitalizing force) and gerontology is close and mutual.

Religious Professionals

Books

637. Clements, W. M. (1979). <u>Care and counseling of the aging</u>. Philadelphia, PA: Fortress, 82p.

This is part of a series of practice-oriented books for minister/counselors, seminary professors, lay leader training, and continuing education workshops. Written from the growth perspective of aging, it includes exercises for facing one's aging through the use of guided imagery and writing oneself a letter, and three perspectives on the use of reminiscence: for recreation, as a shared activity, and enhancing distance or intimacy.

638. Cook, T. C., & McGinty, D. L. (1977). <u>So even to old age. . .</u> Athens, GA: National Interfaith Coalition on Aging, 131p.

A project for aging education in the religious sector resulted in the Project-GIST (Gerontology Instruction in Seminary Training) proposal. This is the final report of the planning conference (February, 1977).

639. Kemper, R. G. (1988). <u>Planning for ministerial retirement</u>. New York: Pilgrim, 100p.

This book on planning retirement for mainline Protestant clergy deals with the specific issues clergy face in retirement; it also integrates lifestyle and financial planning--two major components in retirement planning. A mythical pastor, Fred Mussman is followed from age 55 to 69 as he prepares for and lives through his transition to retirement.

640. Morgan, J. H. (1976). Aging in the religious life: A comprehensive bibliography (1960-1975). Wichita, KS: Kansas Newman College, 34p.

This bibliography was intended in a special way as a resource for directors of retirement programs for members of religious orders. The section "Catholic Orders and the Elderly" lists less than 45 items, a clear indication of a lack of attention to an important subject for groups aging much faster than the population in general.

641. Needham, K. A., Morris, C., & O'Dwyer, P. (n.d.). Self-instructional module in gerontology for faculty in religious studies: Ministry and the elderly. Livonia, MI: Madonna College, 71p.

This is one of a series of self-instructional modules on aging developed during the late 1970s through a project funded by the Administration on Aging, Title IV-A of the Older American's Act. This module consists of two major chapters, "Examination of Attitudes Toward Aging" and "Religion and Aging." An attempt is made to understand influences of the early religious training of older adults, particularly within the Roman Catholic Church. The scholastic or traditional model emphasized God as supernatural being, the lawgiver, and the judge. Commandments and laws were presented as timeless and indispensable. In more contemporary religious thought (which is influencing some elderly) God is understood as present and saving. This personalist notion of God provides the affirmation necessary in late life, although some elderly reject a notion of God which does not entail moral absolutes.

642. Nix, J. T., & Fecher, C. J. (Eds.). (1970). Stamina for the apostolate: A manual on medical care for priests and religious. Washington, DC: Center for Applied Research in the Apostolate (CARA), 127p.

Part five of this work addresses three issues in separate chapters: "The Senior Religious: Renewal and New Horizons," "A Report on the Present Status of Social Security for Religious," and "What We Know and What We Don't Know about the Health of Clergymen." The first of these chapters is extraordinary for its 18 predictions about religious life. In retrospect they seem simply to have been a "wish-list."

643. Payne, B., & Brewer, E. D. C. (1989). Gerontology in theological education. Journal of Religious Gerontology, 6(1/2).

An introductory section indicates the need for gerontology in seminary education and the extent to which it is actually occuring. The second section describes eight innovative programs in a variety of theological institutions. The third section is an annotated bibliography of 133 items. It is intended to serve as a guide for basic library acquisitions on gerontology and on religion and aging.

644. Powers, E. A. (Ed.). (1988). Aging society: A challenge to theological education. Washington, DC: American Association of Retired Persons, 64p.

Scholars in eight disciplines central to theological education contributed to this collection of papers on aging written from the perspective of the expertise of each author. Disciplines represented include: Homiletics (Clyde Fant), Biblical Studies--New Testament (Lindsay Pherigo), Biblical Studies--Old Testament (Kent H. Richards), Pastoral Care (John Spangler), Religious Education (Henry C. Simmons), Practical Theology (Mel Kimble), Worship/Liturgy (Louis Weil), Theology (Lucien Richard).

Articles

645. Albaum, J. (1990). Factors which are related to successful aging in retired Christian workers. Journal of Religious Gerontology, 7(1/2), 71-82.

This article reports a study of retired Christian workers comparing life satisfaction and continuation of activities. A continuity of activities theory was valid only when considering specific activities, namely the religious activities which continue the ideology, identity, and sense of purpose of the individual.

646. Becker, A. H. (1980, Winter). Values and aging. Theological Education, 16, 341-345.

Becker writes that caring relationships are central to spiritual well-being and part of a matrix that includes one's relationship to God, family, friends and the larger community. The author discusses interrelated autonomy, personal respect, contributions, change/growth, and hope. These values are an important motivational core for seminary teaching.

647. Blackwell, D. L., & Hunt, S. S. (1987, Spring/Summer). Ministering to the elderly: A program for clergy. Journal of Religion & Aging, 3(3/4), 139-149.

This article reports a 12-hour training program for clergy on developing linkages between organized support systems serving the aged and an informal support system of clergy. Evaluations and recommendations for the development of similar programs are included.

648. Carlson, R. W. (1985, Summer). The Episcopal seminaries and aging: A survey of Episcopal seminaries and schools of theology as to teaching and training in the field of ministry to the aged. Journal of Religion & Aging, 1(4), 1-11.

This study of 13 Episcopal seminaries and schools of theology found that five of the schools offered at least one course on aging; all schools had an aging component in their pastoral care courses. Recommendations included field education programs that include experiences ministering to the aged, a course in ministry to the aged at each seminary, the inclusion of aging issues within all courses, and awareness in ministries departments that the membership of the church is aging. The author notes that changes have already begun.

649. Chen, M. Y. T., & Goodwin, J. L. (1991). The continuity perspective of aging and retirement applied to Protestant clergy: An analysis of theory. Journal of Religious Gerontology, 7(3), 55-79.

This article lays out an appropriate theory for the study of retired Protestant clergy (a continuity perspective). Another paper in the same issue and by the same authors applies the theory to a group of 185 retired clergy.

650. Frisbey, N. (1987). Retirement of evangelical missionaries: Elements of satisfaction and morale. Journal of Psychology and Theology, 15, 326-335.

This article reports research findings on missionary retirement programs of evangelical missions. The two factors which most contribute to satisfaction and morale in retirement are good health and financial independence (about which 71% of missionaries report concern).

651. Hickey, T. (1972, Spring). Catholic religious orders and the aging

process: Research, training, and service program. The Gerontologist, 12(1 [Part 2]), 16-17.

These four brief symposium papers on Catholic religious orders and the aging process include reflections on research, training, and service programs; leadership training for pre-retirement programs; the aging religious priest; and aging in a religious life.

652. Kaye, L. W. (1986, Fall/Winter). Educating our children about growing older: A challenge to Jewish education. The Journal of Aging and Judaism, 1, 6-21.

The author recommends that education about aging take place in a variety of academic and community educational settings. The proposed approach takes into account the perspective on age found in Jewish texts and secular sources. Included are gerontological training for Jewish school educators, knowledge of the human life cycle, the explication of the life span and aging using a scholarly Jewish approach.

653. Kehl, D. G. (1987). Clerics and the elderly in the contemporary novel. Journal of Religion & Aging, 4(2), 1-20.

An analysis of eight contemporary novels provides the basis for a description of clerical attitudes toward the aging. The range of characters and the variety of their responses is measured, largely, by their possession or not of benignitas, Simplicitas, and Hilaritas.

654. Kraus, M. (1986).   Fear of the evening shadows. In M. Kraus (Ed.), Fear: Issues of emotional living in an age of stress for clergy and religious (pp. 128-141). Whitinsville, MA: Affirmation.

This essay is part of the eleventh annual House of Affirmation symposium. The problems of aging for clergy and religious are sharply drawn; the solutions seem hardly adequate to the problems, although the proposed solutions (self-affirmation, finding role models, broadening our world) may be all that is available.

655. Kvale, J. N., Koenig, H. G., Ferrel, C., & Moore, H. R. (1989). Life satisfaction of the aging woman religious. Journal of Religion & Aging, 5(4),

59-71.

The authors present a nuanced and contextualized interpretation of their findings that strongly held religious values help the elderly nun as she ages and that her responses are different from her non-nun age mates.

656. Levy, W. J., & West, H. L. (1989). Knowledge of aging among clergy. Journal of Religion & aging, 5(3), 67-74.

This study of 140 ordained clergy using the Palmore Facts on Aging Quiz indicated that the clergy's level of knowledge was about that of undergraduate college students. Also noted was a positive bias towards the elderly which may interfere with the assessment of the need for services.

657. Lewis, A. M. (1991). The middle aging of America: Spiritual and educational dilemmas for clergy education. Journal of Religious Gerontology, 7(4), 47-53.

The author notes the considerable attention being given to spirituality and suggests a relationship between the increased interest in spirituality and the middle-aging of America. This raises critical and challenging questions of our seminaries and national religious bodies.

658. Longino, C. F., & Kitson, G. C. (1976). Parish clergy and the aged: Examining stereotypes. Journal of Gerontology, 31, 340-345.

This study of 654 American Baptist clergy concerning their enjoyment of pastoral contacts with older parishioners showed: 1) the majority reported that they enjoy contacts with their older church members; 2) they enjoy teaching adults and young adults more; 3) those who emphasize instrumental over expressive role activities tend to enjoy contact with the elderly less.

659. Magee, J. J. (1989). A participatory residential model addressing the needs of retired priests. Journal of Religion & Aging, 5(4), 53-57.

Roman Catholic diocesan clergy bring to retirement a history of their celibate, hierarchical, and task focussed lifestyle. This article proposes a participatory model of management for retirement residences in order to promote an emotionally supportive, caring environment. The model integrates principles of effective management and group process to ease the abruptness of retirement and the hazard of social isolation.

660. Magee, J. J. (1987). Selected issues in gerontological consultations with congregations of women religious. Journal of Gerontological Social Work, 11(1/2), 187-192.

Consultation with religious congregations of women concerning aging is an appropriate area of social work. The consultant can be instrumental in inaugurating positive structural changes. As well, communal lifestyles characteristic of religious women can give insight about the adaptations of secular institutions of communal living for older adults.

661. McNeill, D. (1974). Learning and teaching experiential theology: An intergenerational journey. Notre Dame Journal of Education, 5(2), 121-142.

This article is a detailed description and analysis of an undergraduate theology course, an integral part of which was a weekly experience of community service with older adults. The course "assumes the willingness of students to share their personal search to understand the meaning of Christian service, compassion, suffering, aging, dying and death in relationship to their visits with the elderly who have had more experience with the personal, social and religious significance of living with aging and dying" (p. 141). Three stages of "ministry" emerge in the process: to (an accomplishment model), with (companionship model), and by (learning model). Reading lists and course outlines are included.

662. Mobley, G. M. (1984, Fall). Electronic evangelists and political change in America: A susceptible population as a bellwether. Journal of Religion & Aging, 1(1), 31-46.

If televangelists potentially have a large audience, how much political influence do they have, especially with older adults? This research article answers this question as well as other questions about religious television viewing behavior of older adults.

663. Oliver, D. B. (1984, Fall). Gerontology in a graduate theological seminary. Journal of religion & Aging, 1(1), 87-101.

This article outlines the model program at Saint Paul School of Theology in Kansas City, Missouri where gerontology has been integrated into the curriculum and degree programs.

664. Oliver, D. B. (1988). Preparing clergy and professional religious educators to work with older adults. Educational Gerontology, 14, 315-325.

The author notes the difference between colleges/universities and seminaries in their acceptance of gerontology into the curriculum. He then discusses obstacles to the assimilation of gerontology into seminary curricula and proposes alternative approaches.

665. Payne, B., & Brewer, E. D. C. (1989). Gerontology in theological education: Local program development. Journal of Religion & Aging, 6(3/4).

This section of a two part study on the role of gerontological studies in the curricula of seminaries reports on the experience in Atlanta of a cooperative project between the Gerontology Center at Georgia State University and three seminaries. Included are a description of the Atlanta experience, and the views of three post-doctoral fellows who served as seminary faculty. The larger section of the volume is a series of nine essays representing a variety of theological disciplines as their authors seek to integrate gerontological concerns into their own subject areas.

666. Simmons, H. C. (1990, February). Ministry with older adults: Sources and resources. Professional Approaches for Christian Educators, 113-116.

This fourth and final article in a series on ministry with older adults focuses on resources taken from the humanities (literature, philosophy, education, history, psychology, theology and Bible). Resources are identified to help those preparing for educational ministry with older adults to enter into the world of the old imaginatively, to engage in systematic analysis, to come to theological perspectives, to reflect on devotional and pastoral approaches, and to select appropriate educational methods.

667. Simmons, H. C. (1989). Presbyterian School of Christian Education: Center on Aging. Journal of Religion and Aging, 6(1/2), 75-87.

This article (like others in this issue) describes a specific program in aging in a theological institution.   As the emphasis of this specific school is the educational ministry of the Church, the article stresses an educational focus (in contrast to a pastoral care focus).   Educational ministry is addressed at the level of the intergenerational church congregation and at the level of those who are themselves older adults.

668. Wolf, M. A. (1990).   The call to vocation: Life histories of elderly women religious.   International Journal of Aging and Human Development, 31, 197-203.

A study of the world of nontraditional women may lead to a reconsideration of definitions of masculine and feminine, to an appreciation of divergent populations, to a study of the never-married woman in retirement, and to an understanding of life history, narrative, and the course of human life.

669. Youngman, B. J.   (1988).   Professional and lay religious leaders' beliefs and knowledge about older people: A short report.   Journal of Religion & Aging, 5(1/2), 93-99.

This article describes the effect of a one day program on 26 clergy and 38 lay leaders.   Based on the Palmore Facts on Aging Quiz, the knowledge of the clergy increased significantly, while that of the lay leaders did not.   Based on the Kilty and Feld Elderly Survey, the lay leaders' positive beliefs increased significantly.   For neither group were negative beliefs significantly changed.

Dissertations

670. Bergman, S. A.   (1982).   A study of ageism-gerontophobia among clergy and lay delegates of the Nebraska district of the Lutheran Church-Missouri Synod (Doctor of Philosophy dissertation, The University of Nebraska-Lincoln).   DAI, 43, 625A.

This study showed that clergy and laity had the same level of knowledge of aging (as measured by the Palmore Facts on Aging Quiz), and had a similar rank order of misconceptions on aging.   Some differences were also noted for the percentage of errors for certain items of the quiz.

671. Bostrom, C. L.   (1978).   An attitude study of selected Protestant ministers in Indiana, aged 50-64, as they approach retirement (Doctor of Philosophy

dissertation, Indiana University). <u>DAI</u>, <u>40</u>, 606A.

This study of 243 Indiana Protestant ministers nearing retirement demonstrated a greater preoccupation with leisure than with work in retirement; concern about adequacy of finances; a preference to live in their own homes in retirement; and that study, work, and volunteering would become viable options only after travel, recreation, and other leisure activities had been explored.

672. Downey, D. J. (1981). <u>Attitudes toward aging and retirement of retired and non-retired women religious in four mid-western states</u> (Doctor of Philosophy dissertation, The Ohio State University). <u>DAI</u>, <u>42</u>, 3255A.

This study of retired and non-retired women religious concluded that retired women religious find their retirement lifestyle a more positive experience than reported in the literature, and that particularly among the non-retired women religious there is a positive interest in the concept of leisure.

673. Evans, L. E. (1981). <u>A seminary field education program in pastoral care with institutionalized older persons</u> (Doctor of Ministry thesis, Eastern Baptist Theological Seminary). <u>DAI</u>, <u>42</u>, 1678A.

The purpose of this project was the design and implementation of a year-long field education program to provide competent pastoral care with older persons in four settings: an acute care general hospital, a rehabilitation hospital, a nursing home, and a retirement living residence. The integration of biblical, theological, psychological, and sociological resources was also sought. Strengths and weaknesses of the program are assessed.

674. Gulledge, J. K. (1989). <u>Influences on attitudes toward old people and gerontological knowledge among clergy of three denominations</u> (Doctor of Education dissertation, Arizona State University). <u>DAI</u>, <u>50</u>, 1768A.

Clergy respondents from three denominations showed a significant relationship between knowledge about aging and positive views of aging. This was related directly to the degree of meaningful contacts shared by clergy and older parishioners. Based on training needs identified by respondents, education programs are proposed for use in seminary training and continuing education.

675. Kelley, N. L. (1978). <u>Socialization for body transcendence: A study of elderly religious women</u> (Doctor of Philosophy dissertation, The Medical College of Pennsylvania). <u>DAI</u>, <u>39</u>, 1870A.

Contrary to hypothesis, a group of elderly nuns evidenced more body worry than a comparison group of 29 elderly secular females. However, caution is suggested in regards to the findings since subjects were not randomly selected.

676. Repka, F. M. (1987). <u>The effects of an experiential group treatment on the life satisfaction of female religious retirees</u> (Doctor of Education dissertation, University of Cincinnati). <u>DAI</u>, <u>48</u>, 611A.

Repka studied the effect of group treatment (involving sharing of feelings, thoughts, and experiences about aging) on the life satisfaction of elderly religious women. The hypothesized positive shift in life satisfaction and the hypothesized positive subjective daily mood levels were not verified.

677. Zwier, G. L. (1989/1990). <u>Expressive and instrumental traits of seminary students in relation to ministry to older persons</u> (Doctor of Philosophy dissertation, Fuller Theological Seminary, School of Psychology). <u>DAI</u>, <u>50</u>, 3261A.

This study of seminary students concluded that those who scored higher on expressive traits also scored higher on "Person Acceptability." Sex, age, ethnicity, marital status, and birth order were not significant variables in preference to work with older adults.

Special Populations

Articles

678. Abelman, R. (1989, September). A comparison of Black and White families as portrayed on religious and secular television programs. Journal of Black Studies, 20(1), 60-79.

This study of the potential learning of the role of communication in family systems noted that neither religious nor secular programs provide information about how to behave toward older people and what to expect from them. More importantly, the absence of older individuals demonstrates their apparent lack of importance in family life. "In regard to religious fare in particular, the absence of the elderly could lead to questions about their importance in religious matters or their involvement with religion" (p. 74).

679. Adams, R. G., & Brittain, J. L. (1987, Spring/Summer). Functional status and church participation of the elderly: Theoretical and practical implications. Journal of Religion & Aging, 3(3/4), 35-48.

This article reports how functional impairment affected church participation of the elderly in a rural county of North Carolina. Impairments studied were in five dimensions: physical health, mental health, economic resources, ability to perform activities of daily living, and social resources.

680. Aging in the eighties: E/SA Forum 72. (1981, June). Engage/Social Action [Special Issue], 9(6).

Although most articles in this journal published by the United Methodist Church are brief, the range of topics is wide: older Americans as resources for advocacy and work, a biblical view of aging, nursing home reform, business and the greying of America, Black elderly, Native American Elderly, Hispanic elderly, and Asian-American elderly.

681. Chang, B. L., Chang, A. F., & Shen, Y. A. (1984, Spring). Attitudes toward aging in the United States and Taiwan. Journal of Comparative Family Studies, 15(1), 109-130.

This study compares attitudes toward aging of Chinese living in the United States with those of Chinese living in Taiwan. Results indicate that young women and men of Chinese descent living in the United States had attitudes toward old people which tend to be more favorable than unfavorable. Taiwan Chinese had attitudes significantly less stereotypical of the old than those of their U.S. counterparts. This study may be important in ministry with Asian congregations.

682. Ellison, C. G., & Gay, D. A. (1990). Region, religious commitment, and life satisfaction among Black Americans. The Sociological Quarterly, 31(1), 123-147.

Using data from the National Survey of Black Americans, the authors study determinants of life satisfaction for Blacks. The study shows that religious participation and subjective well-being are correlated only among non-southern Blacks and that private religiosity is unrelated to well-being. Denominational effects are also noted: non-southern members of traditional Black denominations (e.g., Baptists and Methodists) and southern Catholics report particularly high levels of life satisfaction.

683. Hunter, K., Linn, M. W., & Pratt, T. C. (1979). Minority women's attitudes about aging. Experimental Aging Research, 5(2), 95-108.

The attitudes of Black, Cuban, American Indian, Chicano, and White women toward old age were studied. Important predictors of attitude toward old age were found to be attitude toward death, attitude toward family, and church affiliation.

684. Johnson, C. J., & Hraba, J. (1984, Fall). Life histories and research on

religiousity among Czech-American elderly in the midwest: the evolution of ecumenism and humanism. Journal of Religion & Aging, 1(1), 71-85.

In this limited study of 50 Czech-American elderly from rural Iowa, the life history method revealed that ultimate meaning in life for these elderly is derived not from sectarianism, but ecumenism and humanism. There appear to be no conservative or evangelical elderly among this group.

685. Kimble, M. A. (1985, Fall). The surviving majority: Differential impact of aging and implications for ministry. Word & World, 5(4), 395-404.

While older women are a heterogeneous group, they remain as a population more vulnerable in our social-cultural-economic system. Implications for ministry include the church as a generator of personal and social meanings, the church as advocate, the church and death as the ultimate challenge, and the church as surrogate family.

686. Kromkowski, J. A. (1987, Spring/Summer). Elderly urban Catholic ethnics: Their churches and neighborhoods. Journal of Religion & Aging, 3(3/4), 61-81.

A survey of 65 urban ethnic parishes indicated that while ethnic neighborhoods continue to deteriorate, churches, families and other mediating institutions can cushion the effects of this deterioration. Social poverty, caused by the breakdown of community support will lead to an increased number of neglected, isolated elderly. Included are viable models for effective ministry in these neighborhoods: recreation/socialization programs, informal helping networks, housing projects, non-profit organizations, and multi-parish efforts.

687. Petrowsky, M. (1976, November). Marital status, sex, and the social networks of the elderly. Journal of Marriage and the Family, 38, 749-756.

The widowed, as a group, may not be as isolated from their kin and friend social networks as previous research indicated. Religious organizations perhaps serve as a surrogate family, particularly for widows whose interaction in religious organzations is pronounced.

688. Rowles, G. D. (1985, Fall/1985-86, Winter). The rural elderly and the church. Journal of Religion & Aging, 2(1/2), 79-98.

The author reports research on the living situations of rural elderly and the advantages and disadvantages of a rural context for growing old. The role proposed for the church includes increased accessibility, programs which complement formal services, supporting indigenous support networks, and providing educational programs.

689. Segall, M., & Wykle, M. (1988-89, Fall/Winter). The Black family's experience with dementia. The Journal of Applied Social Sciences, 13(1), 170-191.

This descriptive study examines the experience of the Black family with dementia, the problems and stresses associated with caregiving, the help caregivers need to care for their demented relative, and their coping strategies. A major finding was that Black caregivers of all ages use religious faith as a way of coping with the stresses of caregiving. Caregivers also cited the need for affordable respite services. This finding may contradict the "common wisdom" that Blacks take care of their own at home solely from principled choice.

690. Simic, A. (1987, March). Ethnicity as a career of the elderly: The Serbian-American Case. The Journal of Applied Gerontology, 6(1), 113-126.

Ethnic careers, which may appear to resemble other forms of voluntary retirement activity, help translate ethnic pride into individual pride and self-esteem, and create a sense of continuity, stability and uniformity. Ethnic churches may be a focus of ethnic identity and ethnic careers in retirement.

691. Taylor, R. J., & Chatters, L. M. (1988, December). Church members as a source of informal social support. Review of Religious Research, 30, 193-203.

Examined in this study are the social support networks that exist within Black churches in a national sample of Black Americans (n=2,107). Church members were found to be an important source of assistance to many Black Americans. Surprisingly--although women attended church services more frequently than men, were likely to be church members, and expressed higher levels of devotionalism--it was Black men who were more likely to receive support. This study also suggests that elderly Blacks receive lower levels of assistance from family, church, and others despite apparent and objective need.

692. Tellisnayak, V. (1982). The transcendent standard: The religious ethos of the rural elderly. The Gerontologist, 22, 359-363.

A study from a humanistic perspective of religious commitment in a representative sample of 259 rural elderly concludes that the elderly did not seem to live in a world of unreality. Indeed, despite their very humble circumstances, they were healthy in mind, body, and spirit. The "weight of the evidence points to a hardy, realistic, self-reliant individualism. The elderly in the sample accepted life's hardships with little self pity" (p. 362). The results are not well explained by any behaviorist model; rather Allport's category of mature believers who live by their self-chosen religious goals better describes these individuals. This article is helpful for a review of the literature that shows persistent ambiguities in the area of religion and the elderly.

693. Tripp-Reimer, T., Sorofman, B., Lauer, G., Martin, M., & Afifi, L. (1988). To be different from the world: Patterns of elder care among Iowa Old Order Amish. Journal of Cross-Cultural Gerontology, 3, 185-195.

This article reports the unique ways in which the Amish take care of and sustain their elderly members. In the Amish community, all persons are valued for who they are--not what they do. Offspring care for their elderly parents who may live in an adjacent or connected house called a Grossdaadi Haus (grandfather house). An unmarried daughter, married daughter, or daughter-in-law assumes care for elderly no longer able to care for themselves. The elderly--in fact all ages--are valued and cared for even when their behaviors may cause them to act in unexpected ways. About 5% of the Amish elderly population who are severely disabled or confused reside in Mennonite-managed nursing homes and other mental health facilities. A related article on this theme is "Familial Support of the Elderly in a Rural Mennonite Community" by J. B. Bond, C. D. Harvey, and E. A. Hildebrand, Canadian Journal on Aging, (1987, Spring) 6(1), 7-17.

694. Watson, W. H. (1984). Indicators of subjective well-being among older Blacks in the rural Southeastern United States: Some findings and interpretations. Journal of Minority Aging, 9(1), 39-48.

This study focussed on six indicators of subjective well-being among older Blacks. No significant relationship was found between gender and subjective well-being. Receiving a telephone call was found to be one of the most important factors leading to reduced feelings of loneliness and reduced feelings of being bothered by little things. The study also found "a significant positive correlation between high religiosity and the importance assigned by the older person to staying with his or her family as he or she grows older (r=.89, > .0001)" (p. 45).

695. Wilson, V., & Netting, F. E. (1988). Exploring the interface of local churches with the aging network: A comparison of Anglo and Black congregations. Journal of Religion & Aging, 5(1/2), 51-60.

This article reports similarities and differences in the service delivery patterns of Black and Anglo churches and recommends the utilization of religious belief systems and organizational structure of the churches in the delivery of services.

696. Wimberly, A. S. (1979, Spring). Configurational patterns in the function of the church for aging persons: A Black perspective. The Journal of the Interdemominational Theological Center, 6, 94-105.

A research study of the importance of the Black church to transitions and adjustments of Blacks in old age, this study uses a socio-historical model to analyze the relationship of the church with the Black aging process from the perspective of the Black culture.

Dissertations

697. Berry, B. C. (1988/1989). The global well-being of the older Black woman (Doctor of Philosophy dissertation, Kent State University). DAI, 50, 797A.

This qualitative study found that over 85% of elderly Black women interviewed reported they are very satisfied with their lives. Life satisfaction was uni-demensional with participation in activities, contact with families, and religious faith which motivated them to keep going. Perceptions of health status, adequacy of resources, and mental well being were influer*ial in being very satisfied with their lives in old age.

698. Collier, C. M. (1978). A community study of aging and religion among rural Pennsylvania Germans (Doctor of Philosophy dissertation, University of Massachusetts). DAI, 39, 5012A.

An anthropological study of two groups of older people in rural Pennsylvania showed that for the Anabaptist and non-Anabaptist groups religion and a sense of community function to integrate older people into the community, particularly through secondary group ties and mutual dependence. People in the research group relate to each other, to the community, and in fact to the aging experience through their religion. They are vital, functional, and integrated members of their communities.

699. Miller, E. D. (1985). Elderly females living alone: An ethnographic study (Doctor of Education dissertation, Columbia University Teachers College). DAI, 46, 771A.

An ethnographic study of three elderly women infers that the elderly woman fulfills through religion a) various social functions which meet her need for belonging and recognition, and b) cultural functions, through integration and transmission of certain core beliefs into the different dimensions of her life.

700. Place, L. F. (1989). Priestly people: Aging and continuity in an ethnic community (Doctor of Philosophy dissertation, University of Kansas). DAI, 51.

An ethnographic study of older second generation Croatians who still live in the neighborhood settled by their parents found a high level of individual and collective continuity in their lives, a dense kin-neighbor support network, a devout support of the local (National) church, and a high degree of life satisfaction, grounded in a firm sense of personal and group identity.

Health and Religion

Books

701. Koenig, H. G., Smiley, M., & Gonzales, J. A. P. (1988). Religion, health, and aging: A review and theoretical integration. New York: Greenwood, 228p.

This book tackles the problem of measurement in empirical studies of religion, mental, and physical health. Chapters on religious beliefs, rituals, and experience as related to mental and physical health include reviews of studies and reports on Koenig's extensive work. The authors acknowledge the complexity of religion and its expression, "along with its wide prevalence and potentially powerful impact on health in later life" (p. 170).

Articles

702. Antonucci, T. (1974). On the relationship between values and adjustment in old men. International Journal of Aging and Human Development, 5(1), 57-69.

This article concludes, based on a study of 40 white middle-class males, that the old men who were more adjusted considered work-related values to be much less important than did unadjusted men. A comparison of the present sample with a middle-aged sample showed that the older individuals rated hedonistic values (pleasure, an exciting life, etc.) as much more important than the middle-aged men.

703. Aycock, D. W., & Noaker, S. (1985). A comparison of the self-esteem levels in Evangelical Christian and general populations. Journal of Psychology and Theology, 13(3), 199-208.

This article reports the significance of educational attainments for higher self-esteem levels. The authors note without comment that the "comparisons of evangelicals grouped by age also revealed no significant differences but were interesting in that males and females over 50 years of age have the two lowest subgroup mean scores [...] found in any of the comparison groups, general or evangelical" (p. 204).

704. Bearon, L., & Koenig, H. (1990). Religious congnitions and use of prayer in health and illness. The Gerontologist, 30, 249-253.

This article reports a study of forty adults ages 65-74 who were asked about God's role in health and illness and about their use of prayer as a response to recent physical symptons. Most spoke of God as benevolent but were not clear about God's role in sickness. More than half had prayed about a symptom the last time they had had it, particularly about those that pose the most threat to future health and independence: heart palpitations, shortness of breath, and forgetfulness. Racial differences did not affect frequency of prayer. Those with less education and Baptists prayed more frequently.

705. Birren, J. E. (1985, Fall/1985-86, Winter). Aging as a scientific and value-laden field of inquiry. Journal of Religion & Aging, 2(1/2), 29-39.

This article notes the influence of science on the mobilization of research efforts to improve the ability of the individual to adapt to and maximize the later years of life. Religious institutions are called on to help individuals set goals by finding appropriate metaphors for aging. Examples include wisdom, fulfillment, self-transcendence. In the same volume, Joseph A. Sittler explores the limits of scientific or research models. He indicates metaphors from literature which point to the interior life of the aging persons: the interior drama of aging, the articulated pathos of aging, the silent signal of the pathos of aging, the infinite and implacable diminishments of aging, the exquisite inwardness of aging.

706. Brink, T. L. (1985, Summer). The role of religion in later life: A case of consolation & forgiveness. Journal of Psychology and Christianity, 4(2), 22-25.

Using a case study, the author illustrates several ways religion can help to restore mental health in clients involved in counseling. The seven suggested themes are spiritual fulfillment, confession and forgiveness, moral outrage, behavioral control, acceptance of loss, service provider, and socialization and activity.

707. Cornwall, M.   (1989, December).   The determinants of religious behavior: A theoretical model and empirical test. Social Forces, 68, 572-592.

Religious behavior (personal prayer, church attendance, home religious observance) was found to be more strongly influenced by commitment than by (in descending order) belief, personal community relationships, religious socialization, or demographic characteristics (age, gender, education). Measures of in-group, marginal, and out-group personal community relationships are used rather than standard measures of group involvement.

708. Finney, J. M., & Lee, G. R. (1977). Age differences on five dimensions of religious involvement. Review of Religious Research, 18(2), 173-179.

This cross-sectional study examined the effect of age on five dimensions of religious commitment (belief, ritual, devotion, knowledge, and experience). Age was found to have virtually no effect on any dimension of religious commitment except the devotional practice dimension with which it is positively related.   The authors suggest that older adults tend to increase devotional activity to reduce or alleviate anxieties.

709. Fountain, D. E. (1985, Fall/1985-86, Winter). How to assimilate the elderly into your parish: The effects of alienation on church attendance. Journal of Religion & Aging, 2(1/2), 45-55.

Research on alienation and church attendance concluded that as alienation increases church attendance decreases measurably.   The author defines alienation as a state of being bondless within a social system.

710. Giambra, L. M. (1981, April). Daydreaming, attentional processes, and curiosity in White Americans: Religious, educational, economic, and residency influences for a life span sample. Journal of Clinical Psychology, 37, 262-275.

This article reports the effect of religion (Protestant, Catholic, other but not Jew) and age on daydreaming as acceptable adult behavior, repetitive absorption in a daydream, daydreaming imagery: visual-auditory, daydreams of the personal future, future in daydreams, bizarre-improbable daydreams. This study may help in considering processes of imaginal meditation in old age.

711. Glamser, F. D. (1987). The impact of retirement upon religiosity. Journal of Religion & Aging, 4(1), 27-37.

This article reports a study of 51 industrial workers over a period of six years which brackets retirement. Before and after retirement, average levels of church attendance and belief in God were similiar; however, among individuals there was a polarization of church attendance behaviors. Persons who had attended church once or twice a month reported either weekly or infrequent attendance after retirement. There may be more change in individual religious behavior and belief than would be noted in a cross-sectional study.

712. Guy, R. F. (1982). Religion, physical disabilities, and life satisfaction in older age cohorts. International Journal of Aging and Human Development, 15, 225-232.

The relationship between religious activity and life satisfaction in late life was the focus of this research study. It was found that older people who attended church weekly had higher life satisfaction scores; however, as people age there is a tendency to withdraw from church activities usually because of physical limitations. It was suggested that if regular church contact is maintained through telephone calls or personal visits, life satisfaction may remain high. Responses were in this direction for individuals totally physically limited but maintaining church contact, but they did not score significantly higher on the life satisfaction scores than physically limited individuals having no church contact.

713. Hall, C. M. (1985, Spring). Religion and aging. Journal of Religion and Health, 24(1), 70-78.

This article reports on a wide range of articles which suggest appropriate roles of religion for the elderly. It concludes that religion may be an effective means to counter the negative effects of secularization and industrialization, to identify concerns, and to improve the quality of life of older people.

714. Heenan, E. F. (1972). Sociology of religion and the aged: The empirical lacunae. Journal for the scientific study of religion, 11(2),171-176.

This study of 140 social science journals indicated four major areas of research concerning religion and aging: church participation, religion and personal adjustment, meaning of religion, and religion and death. However there is relatively little cross-fertilization between sociologists of religion and gerontologists. The former, in spite of the importance of death, do little research among the aged; the latter, in spite of their attention to various aspects of the lives of the old, pay little attention to their religious practices, beliefs, or even how these beliefs might help in adjustment to old age and death.

715. Idler, E. L. (1987). Religious involvement and the health of the elderly: Some hypotheses and an initial test. Social Forces, 66, 226-238.

This article reports a study of the relationship between religious involvement, health status, functional disability, and depression among non-institutionalized elderly adults. Although some links are established for women between church attendance and lesser levels of physical disability and depression, the direction of causality is not established. For older men, access to a religious symbol system apparently modifies the link between physical illness and depression.

716. Johnson, D. P., & Mullins, L. C. (1989, September). Subjective and social dimensions of religiosity and loneliness among the well elderly. Review of Religious Research, 31(1), 3-15.

A study of residents of a low income high-rise apartment complex for the elderly, it was found that the social aspects of religion, but not the subjective dimension, was inversely related to loneliness in a significant way. In contrast, the effects of the social dimension of religiosity were overpowered by the effects of depression which was also related to loneliness in a significant way. "The importance of the social dimension of religiosity indicates the need for religious programs and services that will provide a social outlet for older persons" (p. 13).

717. Kart, C. S., Palmer, N. M., & Flaschner, A. B. (1987, Spring/Summer). Aging and religious commitment in a midwestern Jewish community. Journal of Religion & Aging, 3(3/4), 49-60.

In this cross-sectional study age was found to be related to organization and individual measures of religiosity for women among American Jews living in a metropolitan area in the Midwestern United States.

718. Koenig, H. G., George, L. K., & Siegler, I. C. (1988, June). Use of religion and other emotion-regulating coping strategies among older adults. The Gerontologist, 28, 303-310.

Religious attitudes and activities were found to be the predominant coping behaviors reported by older adults in a series of studies.

719. Koenig, H. G., Siegler, I. C., & George, L. K. (1989). Religious and non-religious coping: Impact on adaptation in later life. Journal of Religion & Aging, 5(4), 73-94.

A study of 100 persons ages 55 to 80 regarding the religious behaviors commonly used to cope with stressful life-events and situations showed no difference between religious and non-religious subjects. Stratifying the sample on gender, social class, types of stressors, and amount of life-stress showed no significant difference between religious and non-religious subjects. A small portion (7%) of the sample for whom religion had permeated coping behaviors and outlook on life to a high degree achieved the highest coping scores on 9 of 12 coping measures despite being of lower social class and experiencing more stressful life-events.

720. Koenig, H. G., Siegler, I. C., Meador, K. G., & George, L. K. (1990). Religious coping and personality in later life. International Journal of Geriatric Psychiatry, 5, 123-131.

In this pioneering study of religious coping and personality traits in older adults, it was concluded that there are no personality characteristics distinguishing older adults who use religion for coping from those who use other coping behaviors.

721. Larson, D. B., Koenig, H. G., Kaplan, B. H., Greenberg, R. S., Logue, E., & Tyroler, H. A. (1989, Winter). The impact of religion on men's blood pressure. Journal of Religion and Health, 28(4), 265-278.

This study confirms the interaction between lower blood pressure and the importance of religion. The latter is a more important variable than church attendance.

722. Levin, J. S. (1988). Religious factors in aging, adjustment, and health: A theoretical overview. Journal of Religion & Aging, 4(3/4), 133-146.

The author identifies six theoretical viewpoints on religion and health. Each has guided research. They are activity theory, deterioration perspective, isolation model, disengagement theory, eschatological perspective, and the multidimensional disengagement perspective of Mindel and Vaughan. This latter perspective most closely explains studies of religious involvement. As people age, they disengage from organized religious activities and make up for this loss by an increase in their nonorganizational religious involvement.

723. Levin, J. S., & Vanderpool, H. Y. (1987). Is frequent religious attendance really conducive to better health?: Toward an epidemiology of religion. Social Science Medicine, 24, 589-600.

The authors investigate 27 studies on the relationship between religion, morbidity, and mortality in which religion is defined as religious attendance. They show that there is insuffect evidence to conclude that religious attendance is positively related in a significant way to health.

724. Markides, K. S., Levin, J. S., & Ray, L. A. (1987, October). Religion, aging, and life satisfaction: An eight-year three-wave longitudinal study. The Gerontologist, 27, 660-665.

This three-wave longitudinal study (1976, 1980, 1984) concluded that there is little evidence that the subjects (older Mexican-Americans and Anglos) turned increasingly to religion as they aged. As well, indicators of religiosity were not increasingly predictive of life satisfaction as people age. The authors also conclude that "longitudinal studies that ignore the effect of dropouts run the risk of giving the false impression that religious attendance becomes a more important determinant of life satisfaction as people age" (p. 664).

725. Singh, B. K., & Williams, J. S. (1982). Satisfaction with health and physical condition among the elderly. Journal of Psychiatric Treatment and Evaluation, 4, 403-408.

Noninstitutionalized, elderly people (65 or more years of age) who are more religious--indicated by frequency of attendance at religious services--tend to be more satisfied with their health and physical condition. The subjects in this data group were also better educated, still working, and most were white.

726. Stark, R. (1968, Spring). Age and faith: A changing outlook or an old process? Sociological Analysis, 29(1), 48-57.

This study of the relationship between age and faith (or piety) revealed that "the effect of age on religious experience depends on the nature of the religious expectations for the denomination to which one belongs. Thus the widespread notion that men become increasingly pious as a means to overcome the ravages of time is true only if piety is carefully defined as private devotionalism and belief in an immortal soul. It is not true if the word piety is used as a synonym for religious commitment in its other aspects" (p. 57).

727. Wingrove, C. R., & Alston, J. P. (1974). Cohort analysis of church attendance, 1939-69. Social Forces, 53, 324-331.

A study of five different cohorts spanning a thirty-year period shows little support for any particular model of church attendance as related to chronological age. Cohorts share trends in church attendance by gender (women more than men). Church attendance seems related to the mood of the times, but each cohort appears to manifest its own distinct pattern as related to age itself.

728. Wuthnow, R. (1976, October). Recent pattern of secularization: A problem of generations? American Sociological Review, 41, 850-867.

The author uses a theory of "generation unity" to explain irregularity in the secularization process. A "generation unit" is "a social unit bound together by a common structural location, a common cultural system, self-consciousness as a social unity, and social interaction and solidarity among its members" (p. 851). Using this theory, the so-called counterculture of the later 1960s may have been an important source of the shifts evident in religious trends. Religious trends may not be able to be extrapolated from past experiences.

Dissertations

729. Atkinson, B. E. (1986). Religious maturity and psychological distress among older Christian women (Doctor of Philosophy dissertation, Fuller Theological Seminary, School of Psychology). DAI, 47, 4333B.

This study suggests that religious maturity accounts for much of the variation in coping ability among the Christian elderly. The religiously mature are those who know, understand, appropriate, and verbally legitimate their religious behavior. The promotion of such maturity may improve community mental health in both prevention and treatment.

730. Idler, E. L. (1985). Cohesiveness and coherence: Religion and the health of the elderly (Doctor of Philosophy dissertation, Yale University). DAI, 46, 3493A.

Patterns of religious involvement and health status among non-institutionalized elderly indicate that religious involvement is positively related to all measures of health status. Public religious involvement has stronger associations than private involvement, and more so for women than for men.

731. Kohaut, S. M. (1984). Subjective well-being in old age: An idiographic approach (Doctor of Philosophy dissertation, Bowling Green State University). DAI, 45, 3075B.

This study of subjective well-being in old age concluded, in line with previous research, that income and health are important variables related to well-being. It went beyond previous research in the discovery that these were important determinants of life satisfaction for most but not all subjects. Other notable differences appeared regarding the importance of religiousity, fear of death, perceived control, and social interaction.

732. McGloshen, T. H. (1985). Factors related to the psychological well-being of elderly recent widows (Doctor of Philosophy dissertation, The Ohio State University). DAI, 46, 1710A.

This study concluded that widows who were healthy and active, especially in religious activities, had not worked outside the home during marriage, were not burdened with previous griefs, and whose husbands had died close to home experienced higher psychological well-being than other widows.

733. Powell, R. O. (1985). Values, ego development, and morale in old age (Doctor of Philosophy dissertation, Purdue University). DAI, 47, 802A.

This study of values, ego development, and morale in old age discovered that some values were differently associated with morale according to cohort (and to a lesser extent, ego development). For the older cohort, higher morale was associated with religious, social service, and work/achievement values. For the younger, morale was found to be inversely related to values of contentment and ease, hedonism, and work/achievement.

734. Saul, J. M. (1983). Jewish ethnic identity and psychological adjustment in old age (Doctor of Philosophy dissertation, Boston University Graduate School). DAI, 44, 1642B.

This study of 40 elderly Jewish Americans in Boston found some significant positive relationships between ethnicity and psychological adjustment in old age. The ethnic community offers the aged opportunities for intimacy with like others, a generative role as cultural transmitter, and group norms for adapting to life's stresses. Among the oldest, ethnic identification takes the form of being rather than doing.

735. Schneider, A. N. (1988/1990). An exploratory study of sources of inspiration for inspirational elders (Doctor of Education thesis, Gonzaga University). DAI, 50, 2610A.

This dissertation studied the sources of inspiration for elders who are aging well. The sources in order of importance were found to be ideas, people, things, places and events. These motivated the elders to maintain themselves and their relations with others, to worship, to appreciate beauty, to grow intellectually and emotionally. The predominant goal of these elders was to be active, to reach out, to make a difference. Most believed that their activities and their sufferings were part of a creative purpose greater than themselves.

736. Siegel, M. K. (1976). A Jewish aging experience: A description of the role of religion in response to physical dysfunction in a sample of Jewish women 65 to 83 years of age (Doctor of Education dissertation, Harvard University). DAI, 38, 1536A.

This study of 33 women aged 65 to 83 in a Jewish subculture concludes that home and communal roles, underpinned by a tradition of Jewish values, seem to raise the threshold for physical incapacity and extend functional participation well into advanced age. A further finding related to complexity of world view (as specified by James Fowler's system of faith stages).

Author Index

The numbers following the index entries refer to citation numbers.

Subject Index

The numbers following the index entries refer to citation numbers.

About the Compilers

HENRY C. SIMMONS, Director of the Center on Aging and Professor of Religion and Aging at the Presbyterian School of Christian Education in Richmond, Virginia, is the author of *In the Footsteps of the Mystics* (1992). He has written entries for *Encyclopedia of Religious Education* (1990), and has published articles in journals including *Educational Gerontology*, *Review of Religious Research*, *Journal of Pastoral Care*, *Journal of Religious Gerontology*, *Religious Education*, and *The Ecumenist*.

VIVIENNE S. PIERCE is Associate Director of the Center on Aging at the Presbyterian School of Christian Education in Richmond, Virginia. At the Center she maintains an extensive reference collection of print and media resources designed to encourage and stimulate self-directed learning and to help church leaders prepare for ministry with older adults.